DAVID LETTERMAN'S

Book of

TOP TEN LISTS

and

ZESTY LO-CAL CHICKEN RECIPES

by

David Letterman
Steve O'Donnell

Jon Beckerman • Rob Burnett • Donick Cary
Louis C.K. • Jill Davis • Spike Feresten
Dave Hanson • Larry Jacobson • Chris Kelly
Tim Long • Gerard Mulligan • Bill Scheft
Stephen Sherrill • Jeff Stilson
Steve Young • Eric Zicklin

BANTAM BOOKS
New York Toronto London Sydney Auckland

ACKNOWLEDGMENTS

Thanks to:
Rob Weisbach
Maria Pope
Pami Shamir
Nancy Agostini
Christian Breheney
Jim Mullholland • Michael Barrie

Fred Nigro at the National Bureau of Weights and Measures
who would sometimes come by the office to weigh and measure
things for us.

And special thanks to the *World Book Encyclopedia*, from which
every one of these lists was copied word for word.

•

David Letterman's Book of Top Ten Lists and Zesty Lo-Cal Chicken Recipes
A Bantam Book / November 1995
All rights reserved.
Copyright © 1995 by Worldwide Pants Incorporated.
Cover photo © Christopher Little / CBS.
BOOK DESIGN BY GLEN M. EDELSTEIN.
No part of this book may be reproduced or transmitted in any form or by any means,
electronic or mechanical, including photocopying, recording, or by any information
storage and retrieval system, without permission in writing from the publisher. For
information address: Bantam Books.

Library of Congress Cataloging-in-Publication Data
Letterman, David.
    David Letterman's book of top ten lists and zesty lo-cal chicken
recipes / by David Letterman, Steve O'Donnell.
        p. cm.

    1. American wit and humor. 2. Quotations. I. O'Donnell, Steve.
II. Title.
PN6162.L377 1995
818'.540208—dc20   95-24701
                    ISBN 978-0-553-76357-7   CIP
Published simultaneously in the United States and Canada

Bantam Books are published by Bantam Books, a division of Bantam Doubleday Dell
Publishing Group, Inc. Its trademark, consisting of the words "Bantam Books" and
the portrayal of a rooster, is Registered in U.S. Patent and Trademark Office and in
other countries. Marca Registrada. Bantam Books, 1540 Broadway, New York, New
York 10036.

146684614

FOREWORD

Recently I was invited to a dinner party at the home of Martha Stewart. Here are my impressions of the evening.

1. Decor: Too, too many giant wall-mounted wooden salad forks (eight by my count).

2. Placemats: Pleasant, if pointless, attempt to match color of each guest's car.

3. Party Favors: Wearing crisply starched nurse get-up, hostess administers "flu shots."

4. Guests: Two categories. Dwarflike and loutish. Of the latter, George Plimpton was the worst.

5. Salad: Green beans with ricotta. Tasty. A bit pedestrian.

6. Conversation: Meal-long harangue about electrocuting O.J. during halftime of Super Bowl XXX.

7. House Tour: Cut short by inexplicable noise from crawl space.

8. Main Course: Soft-shell crabs with arugula. "Crab" uncharacteristically dense with bones.

9. Entertainment: Strangely agitated Martha Stewart leg wrestling guests on lawn.

10. Surprise: Small group of neighbors arrive to complain about smoldering tires.

11. Dessert: Cherries with kirsch and sorbet. First-rate.

I thought you would want to know.

Dave Letterman

INTRODUCTION

We couldn't be more pleased that you have selected *David Letterman's Book of Top Ten Lists and Zesty Lo-Cal Chicken Recipes* to be part of your home library!

It is my sincere hope that you find hours of delight and distraction in this collection and bla bla bla bla bla. Okay. We know very well that no one reads these introductions. That's why this space has been selected to communicate information vital to our national security to one of our intelligence-gathering operatives overseas. Badger Two, you are to proceed to Budapest for the meeting with Badger One. There, after a friendly discussion, you are to terminate Badger One. Repeat: Terminate Badger One. Now, what else were we saying? Oh yeah. Book of lists. Yadda yadda yadda. On your shelf and all that.

It is our fondest wish that you and your family enjoy this volume together for many, many years to come. From all of us at *Late Show,* a big "Thank you!" .

. . . and happy reading!

Steve O'Donnell
Writer and Top Ten Enthusiast

TOP TEN WAYS TO MAKE TV BETTER

10. Introduce remote controls made out of delicious chocolate

9. If you scream out the *Wheel of Fortune* answers before the contestants, *you* win the prizes!

8. Slutty red lipstick on all male news anchors

7. Button that lets home viewers give electric shocks to onscreen actors

6. New *60 Minutes* correspondent: Fonzie

5. As you watch, radiation from set gives you a gorgeous tan

4. Something you can hook up to your cat and make it meow *The Beverly Hillbillies* theme

3. Bionic Dan Rather that crushes desk at end of newscast

2. Between midnight and 5:00 AM on C-SPAN, X-rated programming featuring Uncle Sam

1. Three words: The Urkel Channel

TOP TEN SIGNS YOU'RE IN LOVE WITH BARBRA STREISAND

10. You see all history as being divided into two main periods: Pre-*Yentl* and Post-*Yentl*

9. You're in federal prison for gluing a giant wig and fake nose onto the head of the Lincoln Memorial

8. You refuse to buy *People* magazine because you think they ripped off their title from her song

7. You come to after a huge natural-gas explosion and say, "Forget about me. How's Barbra Streisand?"

6. By dating her, you risk destroying your marriage *and* your presidency

5. On driver's license under "Organ Donor" you write "For Barbra Streisand Only"

4. You're doing three consecutive life sentences for killing the video-store clerks who told you they were out of *Prince of Tides*

3. The *Funny Lady* tattoo on your ass

2. Two words: Restraining order

1. You *are* Barbra Streisand

TOP TEN REJECTED NAMES FOR EURO DISNEY

10. Euro Disaster

9. El Biggo Mistake-O

8. Never-Never-Profit-Land

7. La Ville de Guys in Big Smelly Costumes

6. Chapter 11–Land

5. Beaucoup de Crap Américain

4. The Country Bears' Brie & Beaujolais Jamboree

3. Boutros Boutros-Goofy

2. Have-You-Forgotten–We-Saved-Your-Ass-in-World-War-II-Land

1. Ooh-La-Lame

TOP TEN SIGNS YOU'RE AT A BAD *STAR TREK* CONVENTION

10. It's being held at a rest area off the interstate

9. When you count the fake Spock ears in the room, you come up with an odd number

8. Ben & Jerry's unveils a weird-tasting new flavor called "Roddenberry"

7. Dorks with "Moe" haircuts keep wandering in from the Three Stooges convention down the hall

6. So-called starship *Enterprise* looks a lot like an RV wrapped in tinfoil

5. Lack of rest rooms forces you to go where no man has gone before

4. Instead of the Vulcan sign for "Live long and prosper," everybody's giving you the finger

3. Keynote speaker is William Shatner's hairpiece

2. Someone yells, "Beam me up, Skippy!"

1. The hookers all look like Klingons

TOP TEN KILLER-BEE PET PEEVES

10. Plasticky aftertaste when you sting Michael Jackson

9. Dershowitz always tacking $300 dinners on to defense tab

8. That Honey-Nut Cheerios bee—now there's a first-class dweeb!

7. No Killer-Bee Night on *Jeopardy*

6. Other bees making fun of the size of your stinger in the shower

5. "Beard of bees" guys with bad breath

4. Killer windshields

3. Can't sting Zsa Zsa through all that makeup

2. Not one single killer bee in Congress

1. Horizontal stripes make you look fat

TOP TEN SIGNS YOUR KID WATCHES TOO MUCH TV

10. Instead of coughing, he emits short bursts of static

9. Most TV commercials have begun addressing him by name

8. Insists his real parents are Regis and Kathie Lee

7. You catch him putting the cable box in his pants

6. Room covered with giant posters of a shirtless Bob Barker

5. Constantly murdering people in hopes of meeting Angela Lansbury

4. Two words: Remote rash

3. The poor little bastard's got Koppel hair

2. He's six and his ass covers the entire couch

1. He always answers in the form of a question

TOP TEN THINGS OVERHEARD AT WOODSTOCK II

10. "Aren't you the same guy who took a leak on my tent back in '69?"

9. "It's cool how David Crosby can sing with a mouthful of Pop-Tarts."

8. "This must be bad acid! I could've sworn you said Lisa Marie Presley married Michael Jackson!"

7. "There's something familiar about that old naked dude covered in oatmeal. . . . Oh my God, it's Wilford Brimley!"

6. "We want Tito! We want Tito! We want Tito! . . ."

5. "It's a three-day festival of peace, love, and . . . Hey! Which one of you muddy bastards stole my bank card?"

4. "24 bucks for a bag of popcorn?"

3. "Something's wrong with the sound system; you can actually understand what Dylan's saying."

2. "Run for your lives! Rush Limbaugh's in the mosh pit!"

1. "Hey, you 300,000 kids—get out of my yard!"

TOP TEN SIGNS THERE ARE TOO MANY RATS IN NEW YORK CITY

10. Subways have to stop when migrating herds are crossing the tracks

9. On every other block there's a Gap for Rats

8. Often caught trying to mate with the mayor's hairpiece

7. It's practically impossible to reserve a table at any really filthy restaurant

6. Personals filled with ads like: "Furry four-legged cheese-lover seeks mate"

5. Your dinner is being bused away from your table—and the busboy is nowhere in sight

4. Al Sharpton seen wearing one on a gold chain around his neck

3. Vendors charging less for batter-dipped rat-on-a-stick

2. Broadway now just a mile-long river of rippling black fur

1. The roaches are starting to complain

TOP TEN EXCUSES FOR FILING YOUR TAXES LATE

10. Still waiting to hear from Ed McMahon about that million-dollar thing

9. Got nasty paper cut from 1040 form; passed out for three days from blood loss

8. "Tax time? I thought you said *snack time!*"

7. H. Block finished on time, but R. Block was slow as hell

6. Accidentally hired an exterminator instead of an accountant and he used all your receipts to plug up mouse holes

5. Trying to get the lipstick kiss on the signature line *just perfect*

4. "I paid you last Friday. No, wait. That was the paperboy"

3. Think about it: The longer you make the IRS wait for your returns, the more excited they'll be when they finally get 'em!

2. "My friend Leona said I didn't have to"

1. Math is real hard, dude

LARRY KING'S TOP TEN PET PEEVES

10. When my suspenders get caught in the microphone and I'm trapped in the studio overnight

9. Can't interview Dan Quayle without him getting distracted by my shiny cuff links

8. You're about to go on the air with Neil Armstrong and he says, "Please, no questions about the moon"

7. At the CNN Christmas party, Ted Turner never lets me touch his mustache

6. Whenever I go to the Dairy Queen, some wiseass says, "Look—it's Larry King at Dairy Queen!"

5. Stan from Overland Park, Kansas—now there is one five-star dork of a caller!

4. You buy a great-looking pair of Spider-Man pajamas, but when you put them on, they don't give you spider strength

3. Janet Reno always pinching me under the table

2. Richard Simmons always pinching me under the table

1. Walking into a crowded restaurant and realizing it's 90 percent ex-wives

TOP TEN SIGNS YOUR NEW GYM TEACHER IS NUTS

10. All he's wearing is a whistle

9. Warm-ups include jumping jacks, knee bends, and Jell-O shots

8. He's made a nice little home for himself under the bleachers

7. Plays Johnny Mathis records while you wrestle

6. Orders you to hover in place for a ten-count

5. Insists on being addressed as "Cap'n Sweaty"

4. Has class pair off for hour-long make-out sessions

3. Makes you hit the showers after each individual push-up

2. Asks you to spot for him in the men's room

1. Your final exam: Three hours on the teeter-totter

TOP TEN BOUTROS BOUTROS-GHALI PICKUP LINES

10. "Can I can I buy you buy you a drink a drink?"

9. "The nations are united—why not you and me?"

8. "I'm the man so nice they named me twice!"

7. "You'd look *fantastic* in one of these blue helmets!"

6. "I have the complete line of General Foods International Coffees back at my place."

5. "It's not just my name that's long!"

4. "I'm so depressed about the unstable world situation that I really don't think I should spend tonight alone."

3. "In your honor, I'm naming 1996 the International Year of the Babe."

2. "Want to have sex, Madonna?"

1. "Hi there. My name's, uh, Joe."

TOP TEN SIGNS YOU'RE NOT GOING TO WIN THE NEW YORK CITY MARATHON

10. You're losing precious time with your frequent Marlboro breaks

9. They surprise you at the starting line with that rule about "no cars"

8. Suddenly it doesn't seem so damn smart to carry your luggage with you so you can go right to the airport after the race

7. Your three favorite words in the English language are "More pie, please"

6. Before you've gone two miles, one of your four-inch heels snaps off

5. Bad idea to just "duck into" the DMV to get your license renewed

4. You run so damn fast against the rotation of the Earth that you go back in time to when they didn't even *have* marathons and the old-time New Yorkers gather around you and make fun of your running shorts and then beat the crap out of you

3. You get winded licking stamps

2. Instead of the Eye of the Tiger, you've got the Dull Stare of the Dairy Cow

1. You've just finished last year's marathon

TOP TEN GOOD THINGS ABOUT HAVING MADONNA ON YOUR TALK SHOW

10. The host can sit back, relax, and let the censors do all the work

9. She'll frighten any remaining rats out of your theater

8. Two words: Free underpants

7. You get to really break in the "bleep" button

6. For the first time, you truly understand why Sean Penn went nuts

5. Several lucky audience members will get to go home with her

4. It makes CBS executives sweat like fat guys on a stalled subway

3. It's just really fucking entertaining

2. You get to spend more time with her than if you were just having sex

1. It makes your mom proud

TOP TEN SIGNS RICHARD SIMMONS HAS LOST HIS MIND

10. Recently found naked on the San Diego freeway playing solitaire with his Deal-A-Meal cards

9. Loses weight by pulling his own teeth

8. He's suing Clinton for sexual harassment

7. Stays up all night snorting Slim-Fast

6. The other day, he beat an overweight meter reader senseless with a skillet

5. Eats sticks of butter like they were carrots

4. Actually put on a pair of long pants

3. Suzanne Somers found unconscious in ditch with Thighmaster wrapped around her neck

2. Chose Admiral Stockdale as his running mate

1. I see him sweatin', but I don't hear no oldies

TOP TEN REJECTED BATMAN VILLAINS

10. The Ticketmaster

9. Itchy Pants

8. The Pillsbury Psycho

7. Wacko Jacko

6. Little Debbie and her Snack Cakes of Death

5. The Stunned Flounder

4. Lactose Intolerant Man

3. Incontinento

2. The Joker's accomplices: the Smoker and the Midnight Toker

1. The Fry-O-Lator

TOP TEN SIGNS YOU'RE NOT GOING TO WIN A NOBEL PRIZE

10. For the past ten years, your left thumb has been stuck in a test tube

9. You built an artificial heart, but it's the size of a bread truck

8. Your theory of relativity is
   E = MC Hammer

7. You believe that to win, you must be the hundredth caller

6. Closest you've ever come to conducting a scientific experiment: Putting a sleeping friend's hand in warm water

5. You keep brushing off the clumsy passes the Nobel Prize Committee makes at you

4. If you could, you would share the award with your partner, Beavis

3. They just don't have a category for "Shotgunning Six-Packs"

2. Despite all your brilliant ideas, the nurses won't let you have anything sharp to write them down with

1. Title of your doctoral dissertation: "Yee-ouch! Them Pins Is Pointy!"

TOP TEN BRITISH NICKNAMES FOR AMERICANS

10. Velveeta–Munching Hyenas

9. McMorons

8. Tall Muffin Weirdos

7. Dorks 90210

6. Tea–Dumping Psychos

5. Buick Buckaroos

4. Zima–Crazed Savages

3. Gum–Chewing Gumps

2. Matlocks

1. Star-Spangled Ninnies

TOP TEN SIGNS AL GORE HAS LOOSENED UP

10. At state funerals, no longer confused with the deceased

9. Recently seen tapping foot to a Carpenters CD

8. Opens sessions of Congress with "Let's get ready to rumble!"

7. Instead of commuting by limo, straps on Rollerblades and grabs on to buses

6. He's been hangin' with Meat Loaf

5. Taken to wearing a loose garland of daisies

4. Tipper's exhausted, if you know what I mean

3. Shaved head to be backup dancer in Madonna's current concert tour

2. Blinks like it's going out of style

1. Loosens tie during sex

TOP TEN ANNOUNCEMENTS THAT WOULD MAKE THE AVERAGE NEW YORKER VERY HAPPY

10. From now on, every traffic light yellow—all the time!

9. Street vendors should be receiving new pretzels by next fall!

8. It's okay with the Metropolitan Museum if you want to touch the nude statues!

7. Pronounce your cabdriver's name: win a Chris-Craft!

6. Whole city can go on welfare! People in Minnesota to pay for it!

5. We found where that smell's been coming from!

4. If a stranger rubs against you on a subway, you get three wishes!

3. Tap water now available in chunky style!

2. Brooklyn Botanic Garden to expand their rhododendron section!

1. And now, His Honor, the Mayor-Elect . . . Rip Taylor!

TOP TEN SIGNS YOU'VE GONE TO A BAD PLASTIC SURGEON

10. During first visit, he nervously asks, "You didn't see *60 Minutes* last Sunday, did you?"

9. Your nose is attached with Velcro

8. His waiting room is crawling with Jacksons

7. Your new cheek implants feel suspiciously like ketchup packets

6. People always telling you, "Love your popcorn, Mr. Redenbacher!"

5. After a couple minutes in the sun, your forehead melts

4. Paper bags with eyeholes for sale in the reception area

3. Your so-called "bionic arm" looks an awful lot like a turkey drumstick

2. You're a guy who goes in for a nose job and comes out a 36 triple-D

1. Your name is Cher

TOP TEN SIGNS THE GAME SHOW YOU'RE WATCHING IS FIXED

10. One guy keeps getting questions about what he had for lunch

9. You hear the phrase "Come on down, Mom!"

8. The Pyramid keeps "accidentally" toppling over and crushing players

7. During lightning round, player coughs and host says, "Correct!"

6. You see Fabio run the board during Double Jeopardy

5. "Answer the question about the capital of Kentucky and you could be our next Frankfort—I mean, *champion!*"

4. After introducing challenger, host says, "I hope you like Turtle Wax, pal!"

3. Bob Barker has been neutered (*I'm sorry. That's a sign the game-show* host *you're watching is fixed*)

2. Whenever some of the other contestants start to answer, they're chomped on the ass by a vicious wolverine

1. Suddenly Alex Trebek doesn't give a damn whether anybody phrases their answers in the form of a question

TOP TEN SURFER PET PEEVES

10. You catch an amazing wave and realize your trunks have caught a different wave

9. Some wise guy switches the wax you normally use with Folger's crystals

8. Seniors' Day at the nude beach

7. Starkist claiming it's too costly to produce surfer-free tuna

6. People who act all snooty just because they actually attended some of their high school classes

5. Tidal waves that leave you tangled in the Hollywood sign

4. Every time the Federal Reserve gets overcautious about inflation and stifles the economy by raising interest rates, dude

3. The way your sandwich gets all soggy as you paddle out

2. Getting mouth-to-mouth from David Hasselhoff

1. Kelp in your Speedos

TOP TEN SIGNS YOUR TEAM WON'T BE GOING TO THE SUPER BOWL

10. Last year's mascot is this year's quarterback

9. They dump Gatorade over the coach after they win the coin toss

8. Just to be on the safe side, they often punt on first down

7. Inner-ear condition makes it impossible for starting halfback to stay between sidelines

6. Team beaten by local teens in halftime "Punt, Pass, and Kick" competition

5. Incredible goal-kicking mule no longer willing to play for apples

4. Players constantly addressing each other as "girlfriend"

3. They're only giving 109 percent

2. During last quarter, you notice players leaving early to beat the traffic

1. Instead of helmets, halved honeydew melons!

TOP TEN THINGS OVERHEARD AT THE COUNTRY MUSIC AWARDS

10. "Hey, I just found my car keys in Lyle Lovett's hair!"

9. "You know, Mr. Rogers, I saw the most recent *Gambler* TV movie, and maybe it's time to fold 'em."

8. "If Wynonna doesn't drop a few pounds, we're gonna have an achy breaky floor."

7. "Ladies and gentlemen: The weird kid who played banjo in *Deliverance*!"

6. "Damn! Here's your $50. How the hell did you know Johnny Cash would be wearing black?"

5. "You know what's under Garth Brooks' hat? A crop of the tastiest mushrooms this side of the Rockies!"

4. "Now there's an upset! Best Male Vocalist: Snoop Doggy Dogg!"

3. "Somebody help him! He's got a Tritt lodged in his Yoakam!"

2. "*Hee Haw* condoms! Get your *Hee Haw* condoms here!"

1. "I thought 'The Judds' was a nickname for Dolly Parton."

TOP TEN SIGNS YOU'RE WATCHING A BAD DAYTIME TALK SHOW

10. You can't tell the transsexuals from the transvestites

9. *Host* appears in shadows with voice electronically altered

8. Every day, the same topic: "People Who Married Their Fiancés"

7. Whenever host hands the microphone to audience members, they say, "This really sucks!"

6. Guests take turns slow-dancing with a tranquilized monkey

5. Host's cordless microphone keeps picking up police and fire dispatchers

4. Geraldo spends a full hour hitting himself with chairs trying to break his own nose

3. Host pretends he's got a caller on the line by covering mouth and talking in a high, squeaky voice

2. Audience members keep asking, "Can we go watch O.J.?"

1. Host tells every panelist, "Man, you are one screwed-up freak!"

PRESIDENT CLINTON'S TOP TEN RECURRING NIGHTMARES

10. He's at a gigantic town hall meeting where everyone is Sam Donaldson

9. Delivering State of the Union Address in his underpants

8. For some reason, everyone starts calling him "Mr. Dukakis"

7. An echoing voice that keeps repeating, "I'm sorry, the drive-through is closed. . . . I'm sorry, the drive-through is closed. . . ."

6. "Bill, say hello to indestructible Roger Clinton robots numbers one through one thousand!"

5. Hillary passes a three-strikes-and-you're-out law in the bedroom

4. Drifting in a lifeboat with Richard Simmons

3. He's scuba diving and he doesn't inhale

2. Something to do with Al Gore in a sundress and pumps

1. He's in an operating room, the surgeon is Socks—and he's still *really* steamed about being neutered

TOP TEN SIGNS YOUR NEIGHBOR IS A SPY

10. 400-foot-tall bird feeder with a blinking red light on top

9. Bumper sticker on station wagon reads "I'd Rather Be Spyin'"

8. Every Halloween, gives your kids plutonium

7. Excuses himself from cookout in your yard to rendezvous with a submarine surfaced offshore

6. His glove compartment is crammed with fake beards

5. You catch him going through your garbage in a raccoon suit

4. You mention you're having troubles in the bedroom and he says, "Yeah, I know"

3. Says he's turning that stealth bomber in the garage into a Soap Box Derby racer for his kid

2. Always at the Pathmark stocking up on cyanide capsules

1. You tell him you work for the government and the next thing you know you wake up nude in Switzerland

TOP TEN FEATURES OF THE NEW BOEING 777

10. Flapping wings and a big quacking duck beak

9. Just for fun, every seat is numbered "16-D"

8. Every ten minutes, cabin fills with nitrous oxide

7. Seats twice as many as Madonna's bedroom

6. Instead of oxygen masks, bags of candy drop down

5. Super-boingy wheels make landing fun!

4. Recorded message in airsickness bag says, "Whoa! Here it comes!" when you open it

3. Video cameras so passengers can prove they joined the Mile High Club

2. First-class passengers can choose someone at random from coach to be hurled from the plane in midair

1. To make travel more exciting, an "Unfasten Pants" sign

TOP TEN SIGNS YOUR LOCAL 7-ELEVEN MANAGER HAS GONE NUTS

10. Has named his two children "7" and "Eleven"

9. Sleeps in back of store on a big pile of loose Cheez Doodles

8. Claims to be engaged to the cardboard cutout of Kathy Ireland holding a six-pack of Bud

7. Wears a greasy crown of Slim Jims

6. Sells only meat-flavored Slurpees

5. You come in wearing neither a shirt nor shoes, and yet he gives you service

4. Constantly trying to scrub an invisible nacho cheese spot off his hand

3. His freezer case is full of dead woodchucks

2. You catch him in front of the microwave with his pants down

1. Cleans assault rifle while grumbling about "those bastards over at Kwik-Mart"

TOP TEN SLOGANS FOR THE WONDERBRA

10. "The Quicker Picker-Upper"

9. "Looks Great, More Filling"

8. "No More Rolled-Up Tube Socks!"

7. "Does More Lifting and Separating by 8:00 A.M. Than Most Bras Do All Day"

6. "Can Be Used As a Flotation Device"

5. "Much Better Than Our God-Awful Bread!"

4. "No More Bothersome Eye Contact!"

3. "Say Good-Bye to Masking Tape and Staples!"

2. "It's Not Your Father's Wonderbra"

1. "Leave It to Cleavage!"

TOP TEN SIGNS YOU'VE HIRED A BAD ACCOUNTANT

10. His office number is a pay phone at the corner of Forty-second and Eighth

9. Every time you hand him a receipt, he eats it

8. You notice the calculator he's been adding numbers on is actually a TV remote control

7. Makes you slip into a tiny paper hospital gown

6. Keeps pile of coconuts in his office to help him visualize math problems

5. You recognize him as the guy who played "Horshack" on *Welcome Back, Kotter*

4. Only advice he ever gives you is to get them custom-printed bank checks with the cute kitties on 'em

3. Takes you aside and whispers, "Between you and me and the lamppost—a nine's more or less the same thing as a six, right?"

2. Accompanies you to your audit wearing a giant bunny suit

1. Refuses to take calls from an angry Willie Nelson

TOP TEN SIGNS YOUR NAME IS ED

10. Seems like every time you get hit in the head with something, it's right after someone yells, "Look out, Ed!"

9. When your girlfriend breaks up with you, the letter begins "Dear Ed"

8. You look at your name tag in the mirror. It reads "bƎ"

7. You listen carefully as family and friends sing "Happy Birthday to You"—and when they get to "Happy birthday, dear . . . ," you're pretty sure most of them said "Ed"

6. You call up Larry King's show and he says, "Ed in Omaha—you're on the air!"

5. You get married to Roseanne. She tattoos "Ed" onto her butt.

4. Hippies who attend all your concerts are known as "Edheads"

3. The Amazing Kreskin comes up to you and says, "Ed?"

2. You always get a friendly slap on the back and a knowing wink whenever you run into Ed Asner

1. You sign all your letters to *Penthouse* "Jim"

FABIO'S TOP TEN PICKUP LINES

10. "Can I buy you a drink after I finish my 2,000 sit–ups?"

9. "Don't you think the 'no shirt, no service' policy is ridiculous?"

8. "Wanna help me choose a last name?"

7. "You look like a woman who really appreciates a quality creme rinse."

6. "Did you know that 'Fabio' is Italian for 'Fonzie'?"

5. "Mirror, mirror, on the wall . . ."

4. "Do you like piña coladas? Getting caught in the rain?"

3. "How much?"

2. "Why, yes, I am Michael Bolton."

1. "I find you very attractive, even though your chest is much smaller than mine."

TOP TEN SIGNS YOU'VE HAD TOO MUCH COFFEE

10. When you call radio talk shows, they ask you to turn *yourself* down

9. In motels, you don't need the Magic Fingers

8. You're Dan Rather and you deliver the entire nightly news in under two minutes

7. You say things at work each morning like "Did you see that Danny Bonaduce infomercial last night?"

6. You're passing everybody on the freeway when you suddenly realize—you're not in a car

5. You run around your company boardroom yelling, "I've got a great idea! A Disneyland in France! We'll call it Euro Disney!"

4. You jam a fork into the waiter's hand when he tries to switch your regular coffee with Folger's crystals

3. The guy from the Red Cross says, "Hey, pal! Let some of the other flood victims have some!"

2. You're shaking like a Mexican space shuttle

1. You're up to four heart attacks a day

TOP TEN NEW YORK CITY CABBIE NICKNAMES FOR PASSENGERS

10. Dipsticks

9. Curb Monkeys

8. Hail Marys

7. Soapaholics

6. Vinyl Jockeys

5. English Speakers

4. Miss Daisies

3. Turbanless Freaks

2. Fare-ies

1. Potential Spouses

TOP TEN SIGNS LEONA HELMSLEY IS REHABILITATED

10. Counts to ten, then slaps the houseboy

9. No longer seen jumping subway turnstiles

8. Visits elementary schools to teach the youngsters how to cheat on their taxes

7. Is receiving counseling for her mascara addiction

6. Has removed the word "bitch" from her résumé

5. Mumbles, "Sorry" after coldcocking the doorman

4. Always arrives on time for her weekly face-lift

3. All the rooms in her hotels are now free! Seriously! Call 1-800-HELMSLEY right now to reserve yours!

2. Former press nickname, "the Queen of Mean," has been officially changed to "Pookie"

1. She's a hugging machine!

TOP TEN GOOD THINGS ABOUT HAVING THE FLU

10. *Sister Act 2* actually entertaining when viewed with a high fever

9. If you ask politely, mailman will smear Vicks VapoRub on your chest

8. You can use your forehead to warm dinner rolls

7. If you're an actor and you're playing a guy who sneezes a lot, say hello to an Oscar!

6. Sometimes, it's just nice to be clammy

5. Little-known fact: If you stuff a glove with used Kleenex, it'll start moving and talking just like that "Hamburger Helper" guy!

4. Chicks dig phlegm

3. Sickness can give a brief respite from the tedious cycle of travel and watermelon smashing (Gallagher only)

2. When your temperature hits 108, you can bring the thermometer to radio station Kiss 108 and get a free Kiss 108 bumper sticker

1. Two words: Contac Coladas

TOP TEN SIGNS YOU'VE HIRED THE WRONG KID TO SHOVEL YOUR DRIVEWAY

10. Doesn't seem sure which end of the shovel to use

9. Ten minutes into the job, his lips are frozen to your drainpipe

8. He's wearing a bathing suit and clogs

7. You give him a bag of salt and he eats it

6. Says his shovel broke; asks you for vacuum cleaner and extension cord

5. Won't stop bragging about his custom-made six-fingered gloves

4. Prefers the "melt snow with warm breath" method

3. Tells you your wife looks as good in person as she does through binoculars

2. Asserts he knows 30 ways to kill a man with a shovel

1. Doesn't finish till mid-July

TOP TEN LEAST POPULAR ALCOHOLIC BEVERAGES

10. Dr. Scholl's Medicated Tequila

9. Shemp Chardonnay

8. Amaretto di Gotti

7. Smirnoff Chunky-Style Vodka

6. Newark Tap Water (80 proof)

5. Fermented Mrs. Butterworth

4. Seagram's 7, Mets 0

3. Colt .45 That Billy Dee Williams Has Swirled Around in His Mouth for a While

2. Really, Really, Really, Really Old Milwaukee

1. McBourbon

TOP TEN SIGNS ROSS PEROT HAS GONE OFF THE DEEP END

10. Now up to five haircuts a day

9. Has hired a detective to have himself followed

8. Since June, has had four hysterical pregnancies

7. Wants to be called Ross "Dice" Perot

6. Has drawn a tiny face on his finger; introduces it as "My little Ziploc buddy from the TV"

5. Got really drunk and bought Mexico and Canada

4. The tube top

3. Has accused Al Gore of being a super robot sent from the future to kill him

2. Displays a colorful graph showing how he's getting progressively more nuts

1. Has announced his engagement to Whoopi

BILL CLINTON'S TOP TEN NEW YEAR'S RESOLUTIONS

10. Drop Gennifer Flowers from MCI "Friends & Family" plan

9. Prove that Domino's violated Constitution by stopping 30-minute delivery policy

8. Disband Air Force One Mile High Club

7. Push to make "Everybody Wang Chung Tonight" new national anthem

6. Eat an entire six-foot sub live on *Larry King*

5. See if Neptunian Galaxy Masters have any new orders for him

4. Change Socks' litter box daily

3. Change Roger's litter box daily

2. Finally tell Hillary about him and Janet Reno

1. Summit with Ronald McDonald

TOP TEN SIGNS YOU'RE ON A BAD CRUISE

10. Brochure boasts that ship was subject of a *60 Minutes* exposé

9. Captain's hat made of folded newspaper

8. You see the chef trying to knock pelicans out of the sky with a Frisbee

7. Kathie Lee never stops throwing up over the side

6. Shuffleboard with the head of a goat

5. They say they're in Puerto Vallarta, but everybody's got a strong New Jersey accent

4. Passengers must take turns plugging up leaking hull with their heads

3. You keep walking in on Gavin MacLeod having sex in your cabin

2. You go to sleep a little drunk and wake up with an eye patch and a wooden leg

1. It's B-Y-O-Lifeboat

TOP TEN THINGS OVERHEARD AT THE ROCK-AND-ROLL HALL OF FAME INDUCTION CEREMONIES

10. "What a coincidence, Mr. Starr! I played you in the Chicago cast of *Beatlemania*—and now I'm your waiter!"

9. "I hate to tell you this—but you just wiped your mouth with Axl Rose's bandanna."

8. "Jerry Garcia couldn't make it tonight; here to accept on his behalf is a bearded fat guy we pulled in off the street."

7. "Freshen up that blood transfusion for you, Mr. Richards?"

6. "And, uh, a *woove lem drevvels sof* to you, too, Mr. Dylan!"

5. "Accepting for the late Bob Marley is—AAAIEEEEEEEE! It's Bob Marley!"

4. "Earthquake! Oh, wait—Meat Loaf just fell off his chair."

3. "The crowd is on its feet and cheering like crazy! Yes! Linda McCartney is picking up a tambourine!"

2. "I'm sorry. No one under 18 is admitted unless they're Bill Wyman's date."

1. "Run for your lives! It's Elton John's hair!"

TOP TEN WAYS TO MISPRONOUNCE "NEWT GINGRICH"

10. Ging Newtrich

9. Nut Grinderswitch

8. Grinch Neutron

7. Nuke Greenwich

6. Nikita Khrushchev

5. Neutered Lungfish

4. Mr. Goodwrench

3. Nat "Ging" Cole

2. Newtros Newtros-Gingy

1. *NA-GINGA!!!*

TOP TEN GOOD THINGS ABOUT BEING MAYOR OF NEW YORK CITY

10. Only one allowed to spit off top of Empire State Building

9. Every single day: your weight in quarters from the Lincoln Tunnel tollbooth

8. It's the second-most-powerful position in New York—right behind the head of the Gambino family

7. Can't reach something on a really high shelf? Just order one of the Knicks to get it for you

6. Get to hang around Gracie Mansion wearing nothing but a sash

5. Can fix friends' homicide tickets

4. Command performances by most entertaining crazy guys who talk to themselves

3. Any trouble, you just call Batman

2. Full control of secret nuclear arsenal aimed at New Jersey

1. Can save enough money to move out of New York

TOP TEN SIGNS YOU'VE HIRED A BAD HANDYMAN

10. Lets it slip it's the first time he's ever worked with anything except Popsicle sticks

9. Can't lift arms from sides because of Super Glue accident back in '87

8. Identifies flattened cereal box as "solid cherrywood"

7. Shouts, "Look, I'm Moe!" and grabs his own nose with a pair of pliers

6. Claims to be the bastard love child of Black & Decker

5. The EMS operators in your town answer all calls, "Is this about that damn handyman again?"

4. Upside-down blueprint means you're stuck with a toilet on your ceiling

3. You catch him weather-stripping the Mrs.

2. Drinks shellac like it was root beer

1. The only thing he's fixed is the cat

TOP TEN WAYS TO MAKE THE PILLSBURY BAKE-OFF MORE EXCITING

10. Oven mitts full of angry hornets

9. Let the contestants frost each other

8. All recipes must contain both "nitro" and "glycerin"

7. Electric apron that jolts contestants if they break an egg yolk

6. Allow steroids

5. To increase likelihood of thrilling bake-off avalanche, hold bake-off at bottom of snow-covered mountain

4. Philly Phanatic does belly flop onto winning pie

3. Encourage contestants to "get baked"

2. Have that little doughboy "do it" with Mrs. Butterworth

1. First Prize: $10,000; Second Prize: Death!

TOP TEN SIGNS YOU HAVE A DUMB CAT

10. Only seems content when suction-cupped to your car's rear window

9. Wastes eight of his lives in a single afternoon walking into the same electric fan

8. Baffled by yarn

7. Doesn't purr; just makes sound like a stalling Cessna

6. Always confusing "litter box" with "carton containing Mom's heirloom wedding dress"

5. Covered with mouse graffiti

4. Asks to be neutered by Bob Barker personally

3. Seems hypnotized whenever Ross Perot is on *Larry King*

2. No matter what position you drop him from, he unerringly lands on his head

1. Frequently tries to mate with the Dustbuster

TOP TEN REJECTED CAMPBELL'S SOUP SLOGANS

10. "Mmm-mmm Good, If Eaten Before April 1997"

9. "Start Slurpin', Pardner!"

8. "Hitler: Bad. Soup: Good."

7. "The Official Food of Glen Campbell"

6. "Better Than That Lipton Cup o' Crap"

5. "Free Pennies Inside Every Can!"

4. "It's Been Years Since Roy Fell in the Vat"

3. "Sure Beats Raw Sewage"

2. "Nothing's Better on a Cold Day in a Fallout Shelter After a Nuclear Attack"

1. "No Teeth? No Problem!"

TOP TEN SIGNS YOU BOUGHT A BAD COMPUTER

10. Lower corner of screen has the words "Etch A Sketch" on it

9. When you insert a disk, it spits out a pack of butts

8. You have to pedal it

7. The manual contains one sentence: "Good luck!"

6. Only chip inside is a Dorito

5. Whenever you turn it on, all the dogs in the neighborhood start howling

4. You catch a virus from it

3. Screen frequently freezes and message comes up: "Ain't it break time, Chester?"

2. While running, it emits deafening calliope music

1. It cyber-sucks

TOP TEN HOT-DOG VENDOR PICKUP LINES

10. "If you're not a health inspector, I'd like to get to know you better."

9. "I'm a close personal friend of Oscar Mayer."

8. "May I put your change in your pocket for you?"

7. "I wouldn't mind finding one of *your* hairs on my hot dog!"

6. "I'll make you Queen of the Wieners."

5. "Are you beautiful? Or am I loopy on bus fumes?"

4. "Want to go beat the crap out of a pretzel vendor?"

3. "If you let me come home with you, I'll tell you what's in the hot dogs."

2. "You've got pigeon crap on you. . . . Just kidding!"

1. "My franks aren't the only thing that plumps."

TOP TEN SIGNS YOUR U.S. SENATOR IS NUTS

10. Demands that each of the 28 voices in his head should get to vote

9. Demonstrates support for the tobacco industry by eating a pack of Luckys live on C-SPAN

8. Complains that Harry Truman won't return his calls

7. Uses a sword to dramatically sign every piece of legislation with a big "Z"

6. He's the chairman and sole member of the Macaroni and Cheese Committee

5. Pet project: Replacing "The Star-Spangled Banner" with "Baby I'm a Want You"

4. Has saved hundreds of jars of his own urine for donation to the Smithsonian

3. Upon hearing he's been reelected, screams, "Quack! Quack! Quack! I'm the most powerful duck in America!"

2. Keeps inviting Senate pages into his office to play a game called "Pocket Veto"

1. Every evening at dusk, he sneaks into Lincoln Memorial, curls up on Abe's lap, and falls asleep

TOP TEN WAYS TO ANNOY YOUR WAITER

10. Enter the restaurant doing a little dance and chanting, "Chow, chow, chow!"

9. Ask, "Excuse me, are you a really bad singer or a really bad actor?"

8. Make him repeat the specials over and over until the restaurant closes

7. Point to your meat loaf and meow loudly

6. Tie tablecloth around neck and say, "You wouldn't charge Superman for dinner, would you?"

5. "Here's your tip, pal: Steer clear of that O.J. guy!"

4. Demand he feed you with a spoon, pretending to be an airplane coming into the hangar

3. Ask for a Snoop Doggy Bag

2. As he walks back to the kitchen, scream, "He's gonna take a leak in the chowder!"

1. Three words: Eat the check

TOP TEN SIGNS THE PARTY YOU'RE AT REALLY SUCKS

10. Theme of the party is "Come As Your Favorite Member of The McLaughlin Group"

9. What they call "Chex Party Mix," most people call "Styrofoam packing material"

8. Dwight Gooden finished the refreshments on the way over

7. Man on couch near you keeps making out with his inflatable date

6. Brand of champagne: Dom DeLuise

5. As guests stand and chat, host's children circulate among them, slashing their hamstrings with straight razors

4. Guy next to you keeps doing Pauly Shore imitations

3. Guy next to you actually is Pauly Shore

2. You're throwing up; not because you're drunk, just for something to do

1. You wake up the next morning wearing a medallion and there's a note from Al Sharpton that says "I'll call you"

TOP TEN REJECTED METHODS OF EXECUTION IN NEW YORK STATE

10. Craftmatic Adjustable Electric Bed

9. Trampoline and ceiling fan

8. Blind date with some dude named Von Bülow

7. Giant catapult that flings you to New Jersey

6. Lethal injection of Mickey Rourke's bathwater

5. Cartoon mouse shoves a stick of dynamite up your ass

4. Much too much soda

3. Act as own executioner (Colin Ferguson only)

2. Sara Lee Death Muffin

1. Lap dance from Rush Limbaugh

TOP TEN SIGNS YOU'RE IN LOVE WITH JUDGE ITO

10. When you see him on TV, you start licking the screen

9. You buy bags of Fritos and cut them up just to have the word "ito" for your scrapbook

8. You find him guilty . . . of being adorable!

7. In courtroom you shout, "Go ahead and hold me in contempt! Just *hold me!*"

6. You once FedExed yourself to him in a giant crate marked "Evidence"

5. You call Court TV to suggest a 48-hour Ito-athon

4. You move to L.A., open a business called "House of Judicial-Beard-Trimming Supplies," then sit back and wait breathlessly

3. You've declared his birthday a national holiday (*dictators of small countries only*)

2. You're thinking about killing somebody just on the off chance you'd wind up in his courtroom

1. You've completely forgotten Wapner

TOP TEN NASA EXCUSES FOR LOSING THE MARS SPACE PROBE

10. Forgot to attach The Club

9. With all the budget cuts, it was either successful space probe or good office Christmas party

8. Thingamajig on the doohickey musta been on the fritz

7. It got probe-jacked by space punks

6. Should've fed in about another ten bucks in quarters

5. According to the official rules, our dads couldn't help us put it together

4. Must've strayed into Klingon territory

3. Man, were we drunk!

2. Those lying weasels at Radio Shack

1. Mars probe? What Mars probe?

TOP TEN NEW CBS PROMOTIONAL SLOGANS

10. "Catch the Downward Spiral!"

9. "You Can't Spell 'Bumbling Executives' Without CBS!"

8. "Please, for the Love of God, We're Begging You!"

7. "Watch CBS or Mike Wallace Will Bust In on You with a Camera Crew!"

6. "Remember That Alar Stuff That People Thought Was in Apples a Couple Years Ago? Well, We Don't Have Any of That Stuff in Our Shows! Nosirree!"

5. "More Powerful Than the Weather Channel"

4. "CBS: The Other White Meat"

3. "Tune In, Because We Just Might Announce Your Name at Random . . . *Mrs. Johnson!*"

2. "The Shows Are Funnier if You're Drunk!"

1. "Hell—Show Up in the Morning and We'll Give *You* a Show!"

TOP TEN SIGNS NEWT GINGRICH HAS GONE MAD WITH POWER

10. Begins every session of Congress by singing "I Got You Babe" with Sonny Bono

9. Has beaten several Democrats to death with his gavel

8. Now claiming *he* invented the Fig Newton

7. Map on his office wall reads "Newt York" and "Newt Jersey"

6. Has forced supermarkets nationwide to add "House Speakers Only" checkout line

5. Sending a busful of Cub Scouts to conquer Mexico

4. Will allow prayer in public schools—if it's addressed to him

3. Building a vast underground complex full of jumpsuit-wearing henchmen where he can trap and kill James Bond

2. Wants National Park status for his ass

1. The crown

TOP TEN SURPRISING FACTS ABOUT THE AVERAGE AMERICAN

10. In course of life, will eat own weight in Slim Jims

9. Believes in an afterlife and expects to find Budweiser there

8. Has named at least one child after a Muppet

7. Average of 1.2 times a day screams at TV set, "Look out behind you, Magnum!"

6. Feels pretty sure that Ebert could beat the crap out of Siskel

5. Is under FBI surveillance because of unauthorized copying of a videotape

4. If sophisticated cabaret disappeared from American nightlife tomorrow, wouldn't know it. And, if informed, still wouldn't give a damn.

3. Can't stand them no-good, stinkin' Swedes

2. Thinks Thomas Jefferson was "that funny black guy who was married to Weezie"

1. Hates job. Hates spouse. Loves Chee·tos.

TOP TEN SIGNS YOU'VE BEEN WATCHING TOO MUCH FOOTBALL

10. An optical exam reveals a tiny Dan Dierdorf etched into your retina

9. Your grandmother falls down the stairs and you yell, "Touchdown!"

8. Hash marks on your ass

7. You spend all your free time making brownies for John Madden

6. At dinner, somebody says, "Pass the ham," and you hurl that mother 60 yards

5. Your wife wins a hand of pinochle and you dump 40 gallons of Gatorade on her head

4. While making love to your husband, you stop and call for a measurement

3. You're hurled from your car after a high-speed collision and your first thought is, "Oh boy, I'm in a nice tight spiral!"

2. After sex, you spike the pillow

1. When Dan Rather announces a meteor will strike the Earth, ending life as we know it, you murmur, "Please don't let it be Monday night!"

TOP TEN SIGNS NO ONE WANTS TO BE YOUR VALENTINE

10. You've been ordered to be sequestered—and you're not on a jury!

9. Fox is starting a new show about you: *America's Least Wanted*

8. You call a phone sex line and the girls are suddenly all busy washing their hair

7. You get a heart-shaped box full of angry wasps

6. The president declares your love life a disaster area

5. Small print on Paco Rabanne cologne bottle specifically mentions your name as someone it will not work for

4. The Pope asks you for tips on celibacy

3. The babes just don't seem to go for your homemade *Star Trek* uniform

2. The last time you got laid was during the Eisenhower administration

1. You ain't a Gingrich, but your nickname's "Newt"

TOP TEN TED KENNEDY CAMPAIGN SLOGANS

10. "Are You Better Off Than You Were Four Beers Ago?"

9. "I Promise I'll Keep My Pants On."

8. "He Puts the 'Ass' in 'Massachusetts'!"

7. "No Embarrassing Incidents in Months."

6. "I Do More in One Happy Hour Than Most Senators Do All Day."

5. "No Worse Than Marion Barry!"

4. "You Know That Superhunk JFK Jr.? He's My Nephew!"

3. "Vote For Me: the Guy with the Gigantic Purple Face."

2. "Because Everyone Deserves a Ninth Chance!"

1. "Paaarty!"

TOP TEN SIGNS YOU'RE NOT WATCHING A REAL BASEBALL TEAM

10. The UPS uniforms

9. When first inning ends with home team ahead, they jump up and down yelling, "We won! We won!"

8. Instead of bats, they're swinging big rolls of gift wrap

7. Catcher doesn't use hand signals; just yells out which pitch he wants

6. There's a vendor selling jumbo beers to the outfielders

5. From your seat in the stands, you're waved in to relieve the pitcher

4. When umpire yells, "Strike three!" batter looks at him as if the dude's speakin' French

3. Katharine Hepburn is pitching a no-hitter

2. Players constantly adjusting each other's cups

1. Game stops when some lady in a house near the stadium calls out, "Supper!"

TOP TEN THINGS DAN RATHER WOULD NEVER SAY ON *THE CBS EVENING NEWS*

10. "I'm Dan Rather, your Love Anchor."

9. "Here's a report from our White House correspondent, Howie Mandel."

8. "You heard it here first—and to hell with those losers Jennings and Brokaw!"

7. "And now, I shall do 'The CBS Evening News Dance.'"

6. "Critics of the liberal media establishment are invited to kiss my sweet Texas ass."

5. "Anybody wanna buy a fake Rolex?"

4. "I made that last story up!"

3. "Resistance is useless! Surrender yourselves to our new North Korean masters!"

2. "And now, why don't you folks at home tell me about all the news at your house? . . . Uh-huh . . . Uh-huh . . . Uh-huh . . ."

1. "Pour the gin, Lydia. I'm on my way home!"

LISA MARIE PRESLEY'S TOP TEN COMPLAINTS ABOUT MICHAEL JACKSON

10. Always forgetting to put the cap back on the mascara

9. It's always "Liz Taylor this" and "Liz Taylor that"

8. Clutters up the house with all his old noses

7. The bedroom's filled with the overpowering stench of chimp

6. Actually thinks he's "bad"—isn't that pathetic?

5. It's strange—he has the *opposite* of tan lines

4. Chugs a couple Buds, falls asleep on the La-Z-Boy, and snores like a son of a bitch

3. That moonwalking crap gets old real fast

2. I know I'm his wife and all—but the man wants sex morning, noon, and night!

1. He's a great big freak

TOP TEN SIGNS YOU HAVE A BAD AIRLINE PILOT

10. He's wearing a UPS uniform

9. When you take off he yells, "Wheeeeeeeee!"

8. Copilot is sitting on his lap

7. For the past two hours, you've been going straight up

6. Rolls down cockpit window so his dog can stick its head out

5. Keeps tossing firecrackers back into coach

4. Plunges plane from 20,000 feet because he thinks he recognizes a guy raking his lawn

3. Mentions engine trouble and warns, "We might have to rest on a big cloud for a while"

2. You're deep in the Andes Mountains eating human flesh right this minute

1. Keeps referring to the control tower as "Mommy"

TOP TEN LEAST POPULAR MALL SHOPS

10. Gap for Losers

9. Roseanne's Secret

8. Chiggers 'N' Stuff

7. TCBY, you SOB

6. Pricechoppers Clam Clearance

5. Letter J—Only Monogram Shop

4. Just Lint

3. Ye Olde Deadly Virus Shoppe

2. Jesse Helms' Rigidly Old-Fashioned Ice Cream Parlor

1. Pedro's Super-Itchy Swimwear

TOP TEN BAD THINGS ABOUT LIVING LONGER

10. Every time you sneeze, you break your hip

9. More fantasies about Buddy Ebsen

8. Shoulder-length ear hair

7. Seems like every time you turn around, that damn Halley's comet is back

6. Lori Davis hair-care infomercial starts to lose interest after trillionth viewing

5. See *Richards, Keith*

4. You start thinking, "What would June Allyson do in a situation like this?"

3. Tend to get disoriented reading long sentences unless the porcupines get through, Admiral

2. Eventually it's your turn to marry Zsa Zsa

1. All the shoes

TOP TEN SIGNS YOU'RE BEING INVESTIGATED BY *60 MINUTES*

10. Your new paperboy looks a lot like Mike Wallace

9. Your secretary informs you the men are here to install the hidden microphones

8. You don't remember buying the van that's always parked in your driveway

7. You own a sweatshop that's accused of hiring illegal aliens and an odd-looking woman named "Morlene Safer" applies for a job

6. Guy wearing CBS News jacket and headphones keeps emerging from the shrubbery, asking to use your bathroom

5. You're being followed by a car with a "*20/20* Sucks!" bumper sticker

4. You notice your accountant's wearing a brand-new *60 Minutes* T-shirt, sweatshirt, and baseball cap

3. Guy with white hair and eyebrows comes into your crack house and asks in an annoying whiny voice, "Y'ever wonder why they call it *crack*?"

2. While you're lying in bed with Lesley Stahl, she spoils the afterglow with a series of detailed questions about your bank accounts in Antigua

1. Wherever you go, you hear a really loud ticking noise

TOP TEN RESPONSIBILITIES OF FRESHMEN CONGRESSMEN

10. Watch orientation film: *The Wonderful World of Graft and Kickbacks*

9. Wear little beanies shaped like Capitol dome

8. Return Ted Kennedy's empties for deposit

7. When Senate is in session, check Al Gore's vital signs once an hour

6. Run the projector at Clarence Thomas' parties

5. Make sure Cher gets alimony check on time (Sonny Bono only)

4. In preparation for fact-finding junkets, learn all the words to the "Piña Colada Song"

3. Kiss Newt's ass. Then, when finished kissing Newt's ass, consider kissing it a little more.

2. Gerrymander the pork barrels before every filibuster

1. Get fresh drinks for the hookers

TOP TEN SIGNS YOU'VE GONE TO A BAD CHIROPRACTOR

10. Rushes in late for appointment, still wearing his Burger King uniform

9. You have to push aside dirty dinner plates in order to lie down on the examination table

8. Spends hours pushing toy cars up and down your back and making "vrooom" sounds

7. You're fully clothed and *he's* naked

6. Over and over, you hear crunching sounds followed by "uh-oh"

5. While making adjustment, he pretends to pull a silver dollar out of your ass

4. He throws in a complimentary rabies shot

3. Hints that for an extra fifty bucks, he'll "straighten" something else

2. Weeks later, you see a guy on the street selling videos of your visit

1. When you walk, you make a wacky accordion sound

TOP TEN NEW NICKNAMES FOR NEW YORK CITY BESIDES "THE BIG APPLE"

10. "Squeegeeville, USA"

9. "The Unmagic Kingdom"

8. "Your Kind of Hellhole"

7. "The Town So Nice—Actually, It's Not So Nice"

6. "New Jersey's Psycho Cousin"

5. "Son-of-a-Bitchburg"

4. "*Hell-o*, Sailor!"

3. "Filth, Danger, and Noise 'R' Us"

2. "Gateway to Parsippany"

1. "Stickyopolis"

TOP TEN SIGNS YOU HAVE A BAD LONG-DISTANCE COMPANY

10. So-called "dial tone" is just a guy with a kazoo

9. Everyone you talk to sounds like the drive-through window at Wendy's

8. All calls are ten cents for the first minute, $94 each additional minute

7. In the background of every call you make: giggling

6. When you tell the operator you're trying to call a friend in Vermont, she laughs and says, "Hey, pal, this ain't *The Jetsons!*"

5. No matter what number you dial, the same guy answers

4. They insist on being paid with "ass, gas, or grass"

3. Every time you pick up the receiver, dirty gray water pours out

2. They bill you for calls made by somebody named Pepe, and when you complain, they say, "Whatsa problem, man, you no like Pepe?"

1. Their slogan is "Reach out and touch yourself"

TOP TEN ODD FORTUNE-COOKIE FORTUNES

10. Your date will definitely "put out"

9. Skip the pork

8. You will soon marry Elizabeth Taylor

7. That meal you just ate was loaded with MSG

6. Nice tie, dickweed!

5. Help! I'm being held prisoner in a Connecticut garden shed as Martha Stewart's sex slave!

4. Ever tasted tabby before?

3. Everyone in the kitchen has slept with your wife

2. Pay and get out, round-eyes

1. Sorry, pal—those weren't water chestnuts!

TOP TEN DEMANDS OF THE STRIKING BASEBALL PLAYERS

10. Good-bye boring baseball caps; hello festive sombreros!

9. Make it legal to cork their pants

8. Fluffier, more springtime-fresh towels

7. One of those futuristic *Star Trek* transporters from bullpen to pitcher's mound

6. Make baseball cards scratch 'n' sniff

5. Set up bail fund for Mets players

4. Rename infield "outfield" and outfield "happytown"

3. Put an on-deck circle in Madonna's bedroom

2. Three words: Fresh squeezed Gatorade

1. Right to scratch each other

TOP TEN SIGNS YOU'VE HIRED THE WRONG GUY TO PUT IN YOUR SWIMMING POOL

10. Frequently taking swigs from a big jug of chlorine

9. Shallow end: 3 feet. Deep end: 600 feet.

8. Wears inflatable pool toy around his waist at all times

7. Keeps asking, "Where you want the 'gators?"

6. His only tool is a white plastic spoon from the nearby Baskin-Robbins

5. You're discussing the filter and he says, "You mean you don't *want* any hair in the pool?"

4. Ever since the concrete was poured, you haven't seen your cat

3. "That down there? That's the built-in toaster!"

2. You ask for a kidney-shaped pool . . . and you wake up without a kidney

1. Fills pool by drinking a case of beer and "letting nature do her thing"

TOP TEN REJECTED DISNEY MOVIES

10. *Barry White and the Seven Dwarfs*

9. *Mickey's Battle with Helium Addiction*

8. *101 Snoop Doggy Doggs*

7. *The Parent Trap '96*: starring Lyle and Erik Menendez

6. *The Lion King Who Wished He Was a Queen*

5. *Pluto Style*

4. *Huey, Dewey, and Limbaugh*

3. *That Fucking Cat*

2. *Herbie the Love Bug Gets Carjacked by Crackheads*

1. *Swiss Family Buttafuoco*

TOP TEN GOOD THINGS ABOUT BEING THE VICE PRESIDENT

10. After they sign a bill, there's lots of free pens

9. Surge of pride when the Marine band plays the vice-presidential march, "Truckin'"

8. Dan Quayle and Gerald Ford are really easy to beat during "Vice Presidents' Week" on *Jeopardy*

7. Advance copies of all *Garfield* strips

6. President doesn't always eat the entire pie

5. Allowed to pick U.S. citizen at random and spend their taxes on whatever you like!

4. Strange thrill of having newspapers refer to you as "Veep"

3. Those great puff pastries they serve after foreign leaders' funerals

2. Can pat president's ass without being arrested

1. Chicks dig it when you break tie in Senate

TOP TEN SIGNS YOUR KID IS ADDICTED TO GAMBLING

10. Asks if he can double down on some cookies

9. Has converted hamster's treadmill into a crude roulette wheel

8. For a second grader, he seems to know an awful lot about jai alai

7. Changes his middle name to "The Greek"

6. There's a bookie sleeping in his tree house

5. Knows the Vegas odds on where Waldo might be

4. Says things like "Daddy needs a new skateboard!"

3. Wakes up to find the head of his Teddy Ruxpin in bed next to him

2. He's nine and he's dating a showgirl

1. His school lunches are comped

TOP TEN THINGS THAT WILL GET YOU ON THE EVENING NEWS

10. Drink Windex until you see a UFO

9. Announce you're the first openly gay Klansman

8. Sneak into zoo with costume; pose as lovable newborn panda!

7. Become famous in the field of the arts, sciences, politics, or what-have-you, then pass away

6. If you see somebody getting interviewed by a TV reporter, get behind them and wave like an idiot

5. Get elected president and let your wife run the country while you eat nonstop

4. Attract thousands of religious pilgrims by growing a potato that looks a lot like Tom Arnold

3. Ask the Mrs. to cut off your penis

2. Win a game (Mets only)

1. Handcuff yourself to Dan Rather

TOP TEN SIGNS YOU'VE PURCHASED A BAD BEER

10. TV ads begin "From the sparkling waters of Lake Erie . . ."

9. The second you take a sip, your liver explodes

8. For some reason, it's sold in the detergent aisle

7. It was actually brewed by Penny Marshall and Cindy Williams

6. Instead of a wagon pulled by Clydesdales, beer company has a wheelbarrow pushed by a doped-up monkey

5. The company isn't running any sort of sweepstakes, but the underside of the bottle caps all say "Sorry"

4. Tastes more like a mountain goat than a mountain stream

3. Picture on label is of a guy throwing up

2. Your girlfriend announces she's leaving you for Billy Dee Williams

1. When you crack a couple open on a fishing trip and say, "It doesn't get any better than this," your buddies kill themselves

TOP TEN COMPLAINTS OF THE BIOSPHERIANS

10. Bad planning to have everyone in there be named "Billy"

9. On second day, badminton birdie got stuck up in the rafters

8. Cockroaches the size of lawn tractors

7. Bio-toast was usually bio-burnt

6. Truck drivers who secretly deliver oxygen and food in the middle of the night and then can't keep their mouths shut

5. Completely missed three of Madonna's "new looks"

4. They forgot to give us hats, so whenever we wanted to wear hats, we had to fry up pancakes and put them on our heads

3. If the guards didn't like you, you spent the entire time inside busting up rocks

2. Only made one scientific discovery: cans of Pepsi explode if you leave them in the freezer

1. Sick of people calling them "Trekkies"

TOP TEN SIGNS YOUR LOCAL TV WEATHERMAN IS NUTS

10. Uses Magic Marker to trace path of storms on his bare stomach

9. "Satellite photos" look suspiciously like Polaroid snapshots of a desk globe

8. Appears to have the first robin of spring in his mouth

7. Suggests heavy fog is "a good time to stalk"

6. Points to a blip on the radar screen and says, "That there's a flyin' monkey!"

5. Every broadcast he says, "Oh lordy mama! It's gonna rain root beer tomorrow!"

4. Naked except for a little smiling sun cutout

3. The symbol on his weather map for an arctic cold front is a snowman giving the finger

2. Seen checking into Motel 6 with a half-inflated weather balloon

1. Newscast goes long because of his 7,000-day forecast

TOP TEN MARION BARRY CAMPAIGN SLOGANS

10. "Barry: He's Habit-Forming!"

9. "America's Most Wanted Mayor"

8. "Give Me Another Crack at It!"

7. "As Seen on Court TV"

6. "A Vote for Barry Is . . . Um . . . I Lost My Train of Thought"

5. "He's Got a Leadership Jones"

4. "At Least You Already *Know* He's a Criminal!"

3. "I'll Get Drugs Off the Street!"

2. "C'mon! It'll Be *Funny!*"

1. "I Always Inhaled"

TOP TEN SIGNS YOU'RE AT A BAD PLAY

10. The curtain never rises more than two feet off the stage

9. Every ten minutes: intermission!

8. The plot is exactly like last night's episode of *Home Improvement*

7. Marquee has giant "No Refunds" sign

6. Instead of "Author! Author!" audience chants, "Bonehead! Bonehead!"

5. Tony Randall plays the messy one

4. You can read the word "Sheraton" on Caesar's toga

3. Falling stage light gets standing ovation

2. Musical number stops midway through as everybody tries to think of a rhyme for "orange"

1. For dramatic finale, one of the characters says, "Okay, we're done"

TOP TEN GOOD THINGS ABOUT THE BIOLOGICALLY ENGINEERED TOMATO

10. It's the size of North Dakota

9. First step toward the biologically engineered BLT

8. Doubles as a regulation major-league baseball

7. Your blurred vision and dizziness eventually wear off

6. Imagine your favorite pizza. Okay, now imagine your favorite pizza mowing your lawn!

5. Can be grown flat enough to fit in your wallet

4. Will make its inventor, Nipsey Russell, a very rich man

3. Actually shouts, "Hey! I'm getting overripe, you idiot!"

2. The taste? Biologicalicious!

1. Has a nice, firm handshake

TOP TEN QUESTIONS ASKED BY NEW YORK CITY TOURISTS

10. "Does it always smell like this?"

9. "Can you direct me to the emergency room?"

8. "Will we ever see our luggage again?"

7. "Five bucks for a lousy cup of coffee?"

6. "But, miss, why would I want to date a total stranger?"

5. "How do I get to Seinfeld's apartment?"

4. "That gun isn't real, is it?"

3. "Which way to the hookers?"

2. "Why would I want to see a show about singing cats?"

1. "Go *what* myself?"

TOP TEN SIGNS BEN HAS GONE NUTS

10. Has started calling himself "Jerry"

9. On way out of work each day, yells, "So long, ice cream! Daddy'll be back tomorrow!"

8. Latest batch of "Cherry Garcia" contains beard fragments and guitar picks

7. Just got a "lick me" tattoo

6. Has been stalking Mister Softee

5. Walks around nude except for a well-placed waffle cone

4. Recently accused North Korea of stockpiling chocolate chips

3. Daubed a hot-fudge swastika on his forehead

2. In private ceremony, married both Baskin *and* Robbins

1. The Vanilla Swirl Prozac

Jon Beckerman's Uncle Bernie

Louis C. K.'s Uncle Jack

Donick Cary's Uncle Lorin

Rob Burnett's Uncle Milty

Spike Feresten's Uncle Billy

Jill Davis's Uncle Richard

Steve O'Donnell's Uncle George

Bill Scheft's Uncle Herb

Gerard Mulligan's "Uncle" Pete

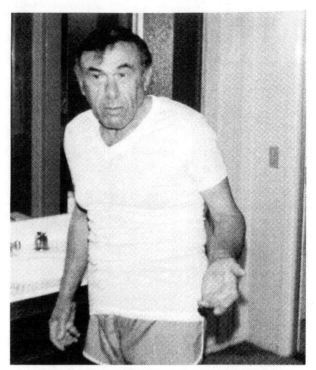

Larry Jacobson's Uncle Howard

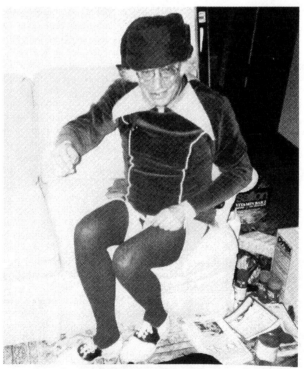

Steve Young's Uncle Bobby

TOP TEN WAYS TO MAKE YASSER ARAFAT ANGRY

10. When you meet him, go, "Whoa! You ain't exactly Omar Sharif, are you?"

9. Introduce him as chairman of the PTA

8. Load his burnoose with bees

7. After he and his pals have been firing their AK-47s in the air, show him your ruined kite and demand five bucks

6. Tell him he'd make a great "Tevye" in *Fiddler on the Roof*

5. Pop a paper bag next to his ear as he starts his car

4. Only let him kiss you on *one* cheek

3. In the middle of the cab ride, tell him you changed your mind and you want him to take you to Brooklyn

2. Short-sheet his head

1. "Hijack" the last piece of pizza

TOP TEN SURPRISES IN A RECENT NATIONWIDE SEX SURVEY

10. Men finished the survey much quicker than women

9. Only 15 percent of ladies are "happenin' ladies"

8. Most common teenage male sex fantasy: a partner

7. The name "Orville Redenbacher" turned up surprisingly often

6. Studies show city workers do it very slowly for many, many hours

5. .03 percent of those polled had sex with the pollster

4. Burt Reynolds had a two-year affair with one of his hairpieces

3. More than 95 percent of all sexually active adults use the word "thingee"

2. Most common sites for sex other than bedroom: car, living room, and Oval Office

1. At moment of climax, 22 percent of Americans shout, "Bingo!"

TOP TEN SIGNS YOU'RE AT A BAD HOSPITAL

10. You go in for routine surgery, you come out with a tail

9. Most of the medical equipment bears the Wham-O logo

8. PA keeps paging "Dr. Jack Daniels" and "Dr. Jim Beam"

7. They don't care about Blue Cross. They just want the keys to your car

6. You notice the framed diplomas are all signed by Sally Struthers

5. Orderly keeps calling you "Spot" and checking you for ticks

4. You recognize your doctor as the kid who was mopping the lobby when you checked in

3. You protest that a can of Dr Pepper isn't medicine and they say, "It's not!?"

2. Every couple of minutes, you hear a bugle playing taps

1. As you're going under, you hear surgeon say, "Man, am I baked!"

TOP TEN WAYS TO MAKE THE SUPER BOWL MORE EXCITING

10. Instead of a football, use a snarling, hissing wolverine

9. 11 players, 10 uniforms

8. Residents of winning city don't have to pay taxes for a year

7. If you go offsides, you have to kiss Dan Dierdorf on the lips

6. Whatever a player's number is, that's how many burritos he has to eat before the game

5. One guy on each side gets a pool cue and a garbage-can lid

4. For final quarter, coat field with that nacho cheese stuff from the concession stands

3. Whenever there's a time-out, John Madden runs on the field in a wedding dress trying to catch a greased pig

2. Complete a pass, do a shot

1. Blimp fights

TOP TEN REVELATIONS IN THE PACKWOOD DIARIES

10. Frequent use of the phrase "va-va-voom"

9. Only 10 percent of taxpayers' money went to Heidi Fleiss

8. Jesse Helms has never seen himself naked

7. Senate pages say "yea" more than "nay"

6. Bill Bradley usually beats the 24-second clock, if you know what I mean

5. Favorite pickup line: "If you've got the ways, I've got the means"

4. Bob Dole was the guy with the long tongue in Kiss

3. Daniel Patrick Moynihan's hat is often used as a birth-control device

2. That "Gopher" dude from *Love Boat* is a sex machine!

1. When he's too tired to go out, Packwood sometimes sexually harasses himself

TOP TEN SIGNS YOU'VE EATEN TOO MUCH

10. Hundreds of volunteers have started to stack sandbags around you

9. You are responsible for a slight but measurable shift in the Earth's axis

8. Doctor tells you your weight would be perfect for a man 17 feet tall

7. Every escalator you step on immediately grinds to a halt

6. World's fattest man sends you a telegram warning you to "back off!"

5. A button blows off your 501 jeans and kills a guy

4. People leaving a showing of *Free Willy* tell you "You were great!"

3. Getting off your couch requires help from the fire department

2. It's several generations before your region recovers from the shortage of dinner rolls

1. Your ears are oozing creamed corn

TOP TEN THINGS CHRISTOPHER COLUMBUS WOULD SAY IF HE LANDED IN AMERICA TODAY

10. "I anchored my ship up here just a minute ago—and now it's gone!"

9. "I claim this trash- and condom-strewn beach in the name of Isabella of Spain."

8. "I've reached India! Look at all the cabdrivers in turbans!"

7. "Nonalcoholic beer? What's *wrong* with you guys?"

6. "Well, I guess I probably *should* have a few more black sailors, Reverend Sharpton."

5. "This is traditional fifteenth-century garb, and no, I'm not gay."

4. "Is there something I'm not getting about Norm Crosby?"

3. "Aieeeee! Giant mouse! Giant duck!" (Assuming he lands in Disney World)

2. "I'm ready to 'discover' a quart of Colt .45 and some hookers."

1. "Take me to Queen Oprah!"

TOP TEN REJECTED McDONALD'S SLOGANS

10. "Food, Folks, and Triple Bypasses"

9. "Maximum Taste . . . Minimum Wage"

8. "Somewhat Safer Than Smoking"

7. "Ronald McDonald Touches Most of the Meat Patties"

6. "Hey, Genius! Don't Pour the Scalding Coffee in Your Lap!"

5. "Over 90 Billion Served—to Clinton Alone!"

4. "Take Too Many Ketchup Packets: Go to Jail"

3. "We Heard That Dave Thomas Guy from Wendy's Dresses Up As a Woman"

2. "Happy Meals: Now with Prozac!"

1. "It's GRRRRRRRRRRRRR-EASY!"

TOP TEN SIGNS YOU'VE HIRED A BAD DEPARTMENT-STORE SANTA

10. After every toy request says, "Yeah, *right*"

9. Charges $5.95 for the first minute, $2.95 each additional minute

8. Tries unsuccessfully to hide the fact that he's wearing handcuffs

7. Keeps sending elves out for more vermouth

6. Whether they want it or not, gives every kid a crew cut

5. He's packin' heat

4. Every day around 10:00 A.M., throws up on the down escalator

3. Instead of Santa hat, wears a German army helmet

2. Tells salesgirls, "Me and Mrs. Claus have an understanding"

1. Encourages kids to give up their toys and parents and go sell flowers at the airport

TOP TEN LORENA BOBBITT EXCUSES

10. Could've *sworn* it was a Hickory Farms product

9. Too much caffeine

8. Fell asleep whittling in bed

7. Those damn super-sharp Lee Press-On Nails!

6. Thought I could exchange it for something larger

5. I was trying to cut the price tag off his new pajamas when he sneezed

4. What can I say? I love a good joke!

3. That's what he gets for hogging the remote control

2. Ginsu-mania!

1. Was tired of playing "Got Your Nose"

TOP TEN BAD THINGS ABOUT WINNING $80 MILLION IN THE LOTTERY

10. They pay you a dollar a year for 80 million years

9. Relatives you've worked years to alienate suddenly reestablish contact

8. Tip a waiter anything less than a thousand bucks and he cracks your skull with a pepper mill

7. Citibank raises the limit on your Visa card to $100 million, and suddenly you're in over your head

6. You immediately lose your credibility as a dunk-tank clown

5. Sure, you can afford lunch in New York City, but what about dinner?

4. You donate it to a college and they name a building after you: Lucky Bastard Hall

3. Overstuffed wallet makes your ass look huge

2. You have to explain to all your buddies in the American Communist Party that, well, you've had a change of heart

1. You know you'll just spend it on 80 million more lottery tickets, you moron

TOP TEN SURPRISING REVELATIONS IN CLINTON'S NEW BIOGRAPHY

10. Rather than Hope, actual birthplace was nearby town of Flipflop, Arkansas

9. Only real father figure he ever had: Janet Reno

8. Even his grade-school teachers remarked on his amazing ability to screw things up quickly

7. As homeroom representative, ordered safety patrol to round up cute girls

6. That time he shook Kennedy's hand, he also lifted his watch

5. Regretted not serving in the military after learning about the free meals

4. While studying at Oxford, got it on with the Queen

3. Didn't inhale, but did eat truckloads of deep-fried marijuana

2. Gennifer Flowers was original inspiration for "Don't Ask, Don't Tell" policy

1. Real name: Bubba Bubba-Ghali

TOP TEN SIGNS *PEOPLE* MAGAZINE WON'T BE NAMING YOU "THE SEXIEST MAN ALIVE"

10. You take a stroll and the local zoo is flooded with reports of an escaped orangutan

9. As you approach the charity-bazaar kissing booth, it mysteriously catches fire

8. You're not only the Hair Club president, you're also a client

7. No action from your pickup line: "I'll bet you've never seen jowls this baggy!"

6. Dictionary. "Doofus." Your picture.

5. If it weren't for getting your inseam measured, you'd have no sex life at all

4. You're asked to be Mr. September in the Guys-Who-Are-Just-a-Load Calendar

3. You wink at a barmaid and she screams, "Eeeeeah! It moved!"

2. People use photos of you as a birth-control device

1. You were buried last Tuesday

TOP TEN COOL THINGS ABOUT BEING IN SPACE

10. A few orbits around the Earth and you're set with frequent-flier miles for life

9. Nobody hassles you about going over 55 miles per hour

8. Easy laugh when you tell buddies, "Hey! I can see Rush Limbaugh from here!"

7. Harder for Jehovah's Witnesses to ring your doorbell

6. Can take a leak right into your trillion-dollar pants

5. Might meet moon babes

4. Really fun drinking game where you do a shot every time somebody says, "Houston"

3. Can give the finger to all of New Zealand at once

2. The Spock ears stay on better in zero gravity

1. Solar-fried baloney

TOP TEN SIGNS THE MANAGER OF YOUR LOCAL GAP HAS GONE NUTS

10. On way into store, you trip over the acid-washed, sand-blasted corpse of J. Crew

9. Shakes the sleeve of the shirt you're buying and says, "Gonna miss ya, Joey"

8. His assistant manager is a mannequin

7. Wears chinos, button-down shirt, and goalie mask

6. His store is crowded with denim-wearing goats

5. When you buy a sweater, he asks, "You want fries with that?"

4. Discovered in back of store having illicit relations with a pocket Tee

3. Declares war on the Banana Republic across the street

2. Tells cashier not to remove the security tag so that when the customer tries to leave the store, a buzzer goes off and they can tackle the person and beat the crap out of them

1. Makes you try on *his* pants

TOP TEN REASONS PUERTO RICO DOES NOT WANT TO BECOME A STATE

10. To avoid spoiling U.S. flag design, they'd have to share a star with New Jersey

9. Alaska became a state, and look what happened—it's freezing there!

8. Don't want to pay Clinton's Piña Colada Tax

7. Too disruptive to be towed by tugboat and welded onto Texas

6. Fear that as a state they would attract more visits from Ross Perot

5. U.S. Mint's stubborn refusal to put José Feliciano on the dime

4. Pennsylvania's already "The Keystone State." And if you can't be "The Keystone State," what's the point?

3. Holding out to become a Canadian maritime province

2. Scary possibility that their towns would get those cornfield "salutes" on *Hee Haw*

1. Might have to sit next to Packwood in the Senate

TOP TEN SIGNS YOU'RE IN A BAD FRATERNITY

10. Every Saturday night is *Dr. Quinn, Medicine Woman* Night

9. Morning, noon, and night spent chugging pancake batter

8. Sound system always blasting John Tesh

7. "Secret handshake" consists of quietly holding hands for long periods of time

6. They proudly introduce you to "Brother Piscopo"

5. The Greek letters are Uma Oprah Uma

4. You organize panty raids on yourself

3. Everywhere you look—poodles!

2. Initiation supervised by Dr. Kevorkian

1. Two words: Zima keggers

TOP TEN LEAST POPULAR CIRCUS SNACKS

10. Chunky-Style Lemonade

9. Clown-Nose-on-a-Stick

8. 60% Polyester 40% Cotton Candy

7. Lobster Boy Bisque

6. Sugar-Frosted Elephant Ticks

5. Stuff Combed Out of the Bearded Lady

4. Stunned Mouse in a Dixie Cup

3. Sackful of Loose Ringlings

2. Wig Squeezin's

1. Freak-Show Cheese

TOP TEN BOB DOLE COMPLAINTS ABOUT HOLLYWOOD

10. In his last couple movies, Brando's been showing way too much cleavage

9. *Casper the Friendly Ghost*? More like *Casper the Bare-Assed Naked Ghost*!

8. Those *Baywatch* babes never seem to get it on with grouchy, conservative old coots

7. Why pay seven bucks to see boozing and adultery when you can watch Democrats for free?

6. In those *Star Wars* movies, could never understand what that Chewbacca thing was saying

5. Ernest won't return his calls

4. *Dumb and Dumber* clearly propaganda for the Clinton-Gore ticket

3. That topping they put on movie popcorn tastes like Quaker State

2. Forget Val Kilmer—let's see Rush Limbaugh fill out that Batman suit!

1. Too many damn Baldwins

TOP TEN DR. KEVORKIAN PICKUP LINES

10. "Can I buy you a last drink?"

9. "Spend a night with me and you'll sleep like you never slept before."

8. "See that guy lying on the floor over there? I did it."

7. "Let me guess—size-six coffin, right?"

6. "I'd love to give you an injection, if you know what I mean."

5. "Hi there, what's your poison?"

4. "If you ever want out of the relationship . . . that can be arranged."

3. "My friend and I have a bet. You're chronically depressed, right?"

2. "Your place, or my van, where I help people die?"

1. "I've also got a *love* machine."

TOP TEN SIGNS YOUR NEW JOB ISN'T WORKING OUT

10. Your office nickname: "Deadwood"

9. Boss' greeting: "Are you still here?"

8. In your one-page performance report, the word "sucks" appears twelve times

7. Coworkers always punching you in the stomach

6. Supervisor says you'll get your next paycheck if you can get all the boys and girls in the world to clap their hands

5. You get numerous prank phone calls for an "Ichabod McPinkslip"

4. You get stung by a bee (*not really a sign your new job isn't working out, but just as upsetting*)

3. You borrow a coworker's stapler and she says, "Just return it before they fire you on Friday"

2. Sinéad O'Connor, who doesn't believe in lies or hypocrisy, tells you straight, "Your new job isn't working out"

1. Your desk calendar doesn't have any months after this one

TOP TEN THINGS OVERHEARD AT A WHITE HOUSE PRESS DINNER

10. "Oh, no! One of Sam Donaldson's eyebrows fell in the chowder!"

9. "Keep them buffalo wings comin'—and that's an executive order!"

8. "Media guys and politicians: it's like a Woodstock for weasels!"

7. "Hey, Quayle! They need more ice water at tables three and four!"

6. "This punch must be strong! Helen Thomas just took her top off!"

5. "Take your hands off me, Senator Kennedy—I don't *need* a Heimlich!"

4. "Take it easy, Limbaugh, those dumplings are for everybody!"

3. "I agree the world situation is serious, Congressman Bono, but the Mighty Morphin Power Rangers are just a TV show"

2. "No, I *wouldn't* like to join the 'Lincoln Bedroom Club,' Mr. President."

1. "I don't care who they nominate—I'm voting for Kato!"

TOP TEN SIGNS YOU'RE WATCHING TOO MUCH COURT TV

10. You hear just one "clack" and you can instantly identify the make and model of gavel

9. After commercial breaks, the judges welcome you back by name

8. All your erotic fantasies seem to involve bailiffs

7. You've rigged up a little Ito beard for your parakeet

6. You have nicknames for each of Robert Shapiro's ties

5. You call MCI and tell them to add Marcia Clark and Johnnie Cochran to your "Friends & Family" plan

4. You can't believe other people don't have a favorite court stenographer

3. Family tells you you're watching too much Court TV and you shout, "Objection!"

2. You can only enjoy sex if you pretend it's a conjugal visit

1. Your kid breaks a neighbor's window and you yell, "Get in the Bronco and *drive!*"

TOP TEN WAYS TO PERK UP THE KENTUCKY DERBY

10. Before race, have the horses drink from a giant trough of mint juleps

9. Have Mister Ed sing the national anthem

8. Horses must run last 25 yards on hind legs

7. Hold it on I-95 during rush hour

6. Last-place finisher becomes part of that evening's "surf and turf" special at Churchill Downs restaurant

5. Winning Thoroughbred gets to do a victory lap dragging a hog-tied G. Gordon Liddy

4. Instead of horses, really fast cars!

3. Jockeys wear nothing but Jockeys!

2. Equip horses with state-of-the-art butt rockets

1. Allow people to bet money on the outcome

TOP TEN SIGNS YOUR SHOP TEACHER IS NUTS

10. Drinks two gallons of marine varnish a week

9. Shouts, "Watch this! You don't need a hammer if you've got a steel plate in your head!"

8. Same project, semester after semester: Make Your Own Coffin

7. Won't go anywhere without first asking the drill press for permission

6. His breakfast: a bowlful of sawdust and wood chips

5. Keeps begging students to sand and buff him

4. Hair barely visible under milky, translucent sheath of Elmer's carpentry glue

3. If someone loses a finger, *everyone* loses a finger

2. Keeps muttering, "In the New Kingdom of Atlantis, shop teachers will be worshiped as gods!"

1. He's built himself a plywood girlfriend

TOP TEN TIP-OFFS YOU'VE CHOSEN A BAD BANK

10. When you make a deposit, tellers high-five each other

9. After you get a free toaster, bank president shows up at your house begging for toast

8. Your monthly statements are handwritten on cocktail napkins

7. They also offer body piercing

6. When you try to make a withdrawal, tellers suddenly don't speak English

5. Your safety-deposit box is a Dunkin' Donuts carton wrapped in tinfoil

4. Instead of cashing your paycheck, they ask, "How about 30 minutes in the back with Rosalita?"

3. You notice chickens roosting in the vault

2. Instead of FDIC, it's insured by Skippy's Bank Insurance & Driveway Paving Company

1. Bank's logo is a dollar bill on fire

TOP TEN SIGNS HILLARY IS THE SMARTEST CLINTON

10. Buys jumbo sack of Slim Jims at supermarket—instead of paying jacked-up prices at the 7-Eleven

9. Always figures out identity of killer on *Murder, She Wrote* at least 15 minutes before Bill

8. Only Clinton who remembers not to eat bees

7. Technically just a hillbilly by marriage

6. Owns a piece of Oprah

5. Repeatedly explains to husband that, no, "Turbo" and "Lace" are probably not their real names

4. Never orders more fries than she can eat

3. When the Clintons appeared on *Family Feud,* she stood in the third position (according to most *Feud* strategy experts, the key position on the team)

2. Came up with Bill's election-winning image as a pudgy, womanizing, pot-smoking draft dodger

1. Her giant, thirty-pound brain

TOP TEN INDICATIONS THAT YOU HAVE NO FRIENDS

10. All your phone calls start with 976

9. You leave your seat belt unfastened just to hear the computer voice nagging you

8. You're still drinking from the same keg you bought for New Year's Eve '87

7. On job applications where you're asked who to notify in case of emergency, you write, "Anyone you know would be fine"

6. Greatest event of your life was being in the audience of a Juiceman infomercial

5. Always referring to "my little buddies, the grackles"

4. Guy who slides your meal into solitary confinement is very standoffish

3. You have a T-shirt that says "I'm Not with Stupid or with Anyone Else for That Matter"

2. James Taylor starts to sing the first few bars of "You've Got a Friend," notices you in the audience, and stops

1. At your funeral, the entire eulogy is "Yep, he's dead"

JOEY BUTTAFUOCO'S TOP TEN TIPS FOR A GREAT VACATION

10. When you pick up chicks at the beach, ask them up front not to shoot your wife in the head

9. See how many dirty words you can make from the letters in your last name

8. Go to a swimsuit shop and grope the mannequins

7. Drop by Janet Reno's place with a pitcher of sangria and hope for the best

6. Show off handcuff tan line

5. Annual Sleazebags' Picnic

4. Volunteer to build homes with Habitat for Humanity—*Nah! Just kiddin'! Get drunk and get laid!*

3. Keep doing really dumb-ass things and your name will stay on the Top Ten lists for years

2. Jet Ski naked and smoke at the same time

1. Put a quart of tequila and a bag of Chips Ahoy in a blender—and thank me later!

TOP TEN SIGNS THERE ARE TOO MANY PEOPLE

10. Constant deafening *whoosh* of five billion people breathing

9. Every square foot of Nebraska is packed with crying babies

8. Alarming increase in the amount of "Sweaty Guy Smell" detected in atmosphere

7. All the good vanity license plates are taken, forcing people to choose really lame ones

6. On dollar bill, a couple of guys peering over Washington's shoulders

5. Somebody married Roger Clinton

4. Average wait for a table at most restaurants now 75 years

3. Surgeon general planning to take warnings off cigarette packages

2. *Two* women now breaking into Letterman's house

1. Gallagher concerts sold out

TOP TEN THINGS OVERHEARD ON "TAKE OUR DAUGHTERS TO WORK" DAY

10. ". . . And over there is the mud we wrestle in."

9. "Overruled, Mr. Shapiro. Ms. Clark's daughter may conduct the cross-examination."

8. "Do the other cabs have brakes, Daddy?"

7. "Chelsea, honey, go ahead and order Daddy a big ol' air strike in Bosnia."

6. "Okay, the final score again: Mets Daughters 8, Mets 0."

5. "If that little brat snaps my suspenders one more time, you'll be an *ex*-employee of *Larry King Live!*"

4. "Hurry up, sweetie. Just cock the hammer and fire at the bad guy."

3. "Here's $50,000 in cash, Senator . . . and, heh-heh, here's a dollar bill for you, too, little girl!"

2. *INSERT YOUR OWN WOODY ALLEN JOKE HERE*

1. "Dad, are you sure this Mickey Mouse costume is big enough for both of us?"

TOP TEN PERKS OF WINNING THE STANLEY CUP

10. Take it into any Baskin-Robbins and they have to fill it with ice cream—no questions asked!

9. Ideal for storing those knocked-out teeth

8. When jammed into your steering wheel, Stanley Cup works better than The Club

7. For one full year, people have to call you "Stanley"

6. Legal for you to wear skates while driving

5. Harder for other teams to score goals with that giant cup in the crease

4. Fifty free stitches from the doctor of your choice

3. Weekend use of Marv Albert's hair

2. Cup tail

1. My friend, you can't drink beer out of a Nobel Prize!

TOP TEN SIGNS THE GUY MUGGING YOU HAS NEVER MUGGED BEFORE

10. In addition to wearing a ski mask, he's got ski poles and skis

9. Announces, "This is a nugging"

8. Asks you to hold his gun while he puts on some Chap Stick

7. You're a policeman in full uniform standing right in front of the station house surrounded by fellow officers carrying assault rifles

6. Wears paper hat that says "Trainee"

5. Warns, "Don't make me use this realistic-looking squirt gun!"

4. He keeps murmuring, "So this is it! Now McGruff and I are mortal foes!"

3. Makes getaway in limo with license-plate number TRUMP-1

2. When he's done, he says, "That was fun! Now you mug me!"

1. During police lineup, he waves to you and shouts, "Remember me?"

TOP TEN THINGS THAT WILL GET YOU KICKED OUT OF A BOOKSTORE

10. Sneak up behind someone reading a romance novel and make kissing noises

9. Throw a book-signing party—even though you haven't written a book

8. Lick cookbook, pause, shake your head, and move on to the next one

7. Carry out a stack of Shirley MacLaine's books; tell clerk you paid for them in a previous life

6. Shout really loudly, "Hey look, everybody! 'Penis' is in the dictionary!"

5. Ask if there's a Books on Tape version of *Mein Kampf* read by Carol Channing

4. Sweep the science-fiction books off the shelf and scream, "Nothing but Earthling lies!"

3. Return copy of the Bible; say you couldn't find Waldo in it anywhere

2. Loudly announce you have naked photos of Nancy Drew

1. Push over bookshelves like giant dominoes

TOP TEN OTHER REASONS PEOPLE ARE SUING McDONALD'S

10. Red clown hairs found on the apple pies

9. When patrons ask for a couple extra napkins, they're routinely blasted with high-intensity tear gas

8. One in every fifty McNuggets has a pink, cordlike tail

7. If you pour one of those milkshakes into a copper cylinder, superheat it to 1,000 degrees, and then dump it on yourself—brother, that can hurt!

6. You know them fancy french fries? Them boys ain't exactly comin' from France!

5. Mayor McCheese secretly videotaped in hotel room smoking ketchup-flavored crack

4. The secret of "Secret Sauce"? A little something called Vicks VapoRub

3. Grimace keeps breaking into furniture stores and trying to mate with the beanbag chairs

2. "Happy Meal" may induce violent mood swings

1. A woman from Delaware ate three Big Macs at one sitting and her ass inflated so rapidly that her car turned over

TOP TEN THINGS OVERHEARD AT THE ACADEMY AWARDS

10. "That's cute. Siskel's sitting on Ebert's lap."

9. "Wow! Brando really gives new meaning to the term 'seat-filler'!"

8. "Will that be snubbing or nonsnubbing, Miss Streisand?"

7. "And now, a musical tribute to the films of Pauly Shore!"

6. "Good evening, Mr. Stallone. Uh, what are you doing here?"

5. "Just since this ceremony started, Don Johnson and Melanie Griffith have been married and divorced again three times!"

4. "I'm Oliver Stone, and I'm here to tell you a vast international conspiracy has caused the men's room to run out of paper towels!"

3. "Hey, look! Price and Waterhouse are gettin' it on!"

2. "Here to present the award for special effects, the reanimated corpse of Orson Welles!"

1. "And the winner is—*owww!* Paper cut!"

TOP TEN EASTER BUNNY PICKUP LINES

10. "Ever done it on a pile of artificial grass?"

9. "I'm being managed by Don King again."

8. "Relax! I'm just hiding an egg."

7. "My foot isn't the only part of me that's lucky!"

6. "I can get you free makeup. I did some product testing for Revlon."

5. "I'm in the mood to multiply."

4. "Come to anti-fur rallies often?"

3. "You're not Jewish, are you?"

2. "That ain't a carrot."

1. "Would you mind checking me for ear mites?"

HILLARY CLINTON'S TOP TEN TIPS FOR MAKING YOUR MAN HAPPY

10. Barbecue-flavored lip gloss

9. Lean close, put your mouth to his ear, and whisper, "Bubbaaaaaa"

8. Take him away for a quiet weekend of taxing and spending

7. Point out how fat William Howard Taft was. 340 pounds! Now, *that's* a fat president!

6. Spend plenty of time inside the Beltway, if you know what I mean

5. If he wants to be called "Captain Picard," call him "Captain Picard." Who the hell's gonna find out?

4. Air Force One Mile High Club

3. Every once in a while, let *him* run the country

2. Don't admit how cute you think the last couple of newly-discovered half brothers are

1. Every morning, send him off with "Get out there and *waffle*, Tiger!"

TOP TEN SIGNS SOMETHING IS VERY, VERY WRONG UP AT PEPPERIDGE FARM

10. That old guy with the New England accent from the commercials? He licks all the cookies before packaging.

9. Only thing they've produced in the last three months is a two-mile-long Mint Milano

8. Keebler elves being held hostage in an abandoned silo

7. The Goldfish crackers taste like actual goldfish

6. Employees have been walking around naked except for straw boaters

5. You call their 800 information number and all you hear is someone breathing heavily and repeating, "Croutons . . . croutons . . . croutons . . ."

4. The new Raspberry Mansons

3. Assortment of Old-Fashioned Tea Biscuits now includes a vial of crack

2. Anatomically correct gingerbread men

1. Openly admit it's not a "farm" but an armed compound full of sugar-crazed fanatics

TOP TEN COMPLAINTS OF DAVE LETTERMAN'S SECRETARY

10. Always using her White-Out to paint his fingernails

9. Strict "no talking" policy during *The Montel Williams Show*

8. About 300 times a day, buzzes her on the intercom and shouts, "Breaker, breaker, good buddy!"

7. The weird "eggy" smell

6. Insists on filling every inch of open space with more photos of Cody and Cassidy

5. Frequently forgets to fasten the back of his hospital gown

4. Very time-consuming to forge realistic new fan mail every day

3. Office walls black and greasy from the pig roasts

2. When he's out of town, has that woman break into his *secretary's* house

1. Crying jags when he's listening to his Swiss music boxes

TOP TEN WAYS TO TELL YOU'RE AT A BAD AIRPORT

10. "Control tower" just a guy with a bullhorn on a stepladder

9. Runway littered with stripped Chevys

8. Technician asks if he can borrow your cup of coffee to "de-ice" a 747

7. Gift shop selling items from your just-checked luggage

6. Guard at metal detector asks you to turn your head and cough

5. Lost children get to bawl into the PA system until somebody comes to claim them

4. All flights are either going to or arriving from Saskatoon, Canada

3. Only car rental company is "Louie's '78 Monte Carlo"

2. A lot of arriving passengers appear to be dragging parachutes

1. You see someone preboarding a flight attendant

TOP TEN TIP-OFFS THAT SOMETHING IS WRONG WITH YOUR SCHOOL LUNCH

10. The surprise in the "Vegetable Surprise" is a nasty case of botulism

9. Tapioca multiplies by splitting apart into two new tapiocas

8. You see a lunch lady straining spaghetti through her hair net

7. A slew of white lab mice disappear and for weeks they're serving albino pot pies

6. Robert Shapiro shows up to order DNA testing on it

5. They proudly grow their own mushrooms in the gym shower

4. Gravy forms a skull and crossbones in the mashed potatoes

3. When you say the name "Steve," your rice pudding shudders violently as if to say, "Yes—that's me. My name's Steve!"

2. Chicken à la Don King

1. Occasionally see rats stagger out of the kitchen and collapse

TOP TEN WAYS TO MAKE MADONNA ANGRY

10. Sit in front row at her concert; knit

9. Tell her you love the way she turns the letters on *Wheel of Fortune*

8. Every time she sings "Like a Virgin," shout, "Yeah, *right!*"

7. Ben-Gay in the cone bra

6. Bang on door while she's in bathroom and yell, "What're you doing in there? Reinventing yourself?"

5. Doze off during sex with her

4. Vogue before 5:00 P.M.

3. Keep asking for your old coffeemaker back (Sean Penn only)

2. Refer to her breasts as "Jacoby" and "Meyers"

1. Tell her, "You're no Juice Newton"

TOP TEN SIGNS YOUR SHOE SALESMAN IS THE DEVIL

10. All shoe sizes are 666

9. Offers you 15 percent discount if you trade in your soul

8. The whole wingtip section stinks of brimstone

7. To get the pumps in the color you want, says he might have to send back to hell for them

6. Instead of Dr. Scholl's foot-care products, he carries Dr. Mengele's

5. Asks, "So what's your cloven hoof size?"

4. Sign out front reads "Visa, MasterCard, and Abandon All Hope Ye Who Enter Here"

3. When you tell him you don't like a pair of shoes, he spits pea soup at you

2. Mentions he just bought a similar pair of these tasseled loafers for his buddy Hitler

1. When Michael Jackson got married, his shoe store froze over

TOP TEN SIGNS THAT YOU'RE NOT GOING TO WIN THE MISS AMERICA PAGEANT

10. Instead of putting Vaseline on your teeth, you use chunky peanut butter

9. You're Miss New York and your talent is giving the finger

8. After your musical number, Regis turns to Kathie Lee and says, "Wow! That really sucked!"

7. Your flask is bulging under your evening gown

6. During the interview portion, you announce the man you most admire is your pimp

5. Someone's replaced your "Miss Kentucky" sash with one that reads "Sanitized for your protection"

4. Stunned silence when you finish your act: draining a jar of mayonnaise with a straw

3. You're an anteater and you notice all the judges are ants! (Crazy Cartoon World Miss America Pageant only)

2. You're pretty, but there's no getting around the fact that your name is Carl and you're a longshoreman

1. Officials discover you've corked your bra

TOP TEN WAYS NEW YORK CITY IS CUTTING BACK

10. Combining the Christmas and Easter garbage pickups

 9. City will stop sandblasting and repainting Leona Helmsley

 8. U–Drive–Em subway trains

 7. No more pension plan for hookers

 6. Brooklyn Bridge now ends 75 feet short of Brooklyn

 5. Eliminating Rikers Island Senior Prom

 4. Grade schoolers only learning letters *A* through *K*

 3. Calling 911 is now $3.99 for the first minute, $2.99 each additional minute

 2. Only one pantsless psycho per city block

 1. Sorry, pardners—but from now on, Queens is on its own

TOP TEN DISTURBING EXAMPLES OF VIOLENCE ON TV

10. Kathie Lee kicks Regis in the ass

9. Disgruntled Postal Worker Week on *Jeopardy*

8. Malfunctioning Thighmaster beheads Suzanne Somers

7. The day an obviously drunk Jacques Cousteau beat up a manatee

6. Half-hour Ross Perot infomercial where he bites the heads off mice

5. Weatherman Willard Scott points to a storm front and it snaps his arm off

4. Reporters at White House function get between Clinton and the buffet

3. Talking finger from the Ziploc commercials chopped off by terrified housewife

2. Richard Simmons tries to hug a fat guy who knocks him unconscious with a two-by-four

1. Special episode of *Family Matters* where everybody gets stranded on a desert island and Urkel is killed for meat

TOP TEN TIP-OFFS TO GUYS: YOU'RE ON A BAD DATE

10. She whispers to waiter, "Please kill me"

9. Doesn't laugh when you give yourself ketchup sideburns

8. All she wants to talk about is how great it is working for Heidi Fleiss

7. It's been four hours since she left for the ladies' room

6. You catch her giving her phone number to the guy squeegeeing your windshield

5. Lunges at you several times with a steak knife

4. She keeps calling you "Bachelor Number Three" when she knows *damn well* that you're Bachelor Number Two!

3. Suggests you get back together with her mother, Mia

2. Seems shocked rather than delighted when you show up at her door sporting a thick, buzzing beard of bees

1. "Whoa! Is it 8:15 already!?"

TOP TEN TIP-OFFS TO WOMEN: YOU'RE ON A BAD DATE

10. You order a Double Whopper and he says, "Hey, my name ain't Rockefeller, honey"

9. You have never heard anyone speak at such length and with such intensity about an ant farm

8. Seems to know an awful lot about your shower routine

7. Your dinner reservations are under "Loser, 2"

6. He gets really angry when you tell him you like his Siamese twin brother better

5. He's proud of how long he can sustain a burp

4. You check a dozen encyclopedias and almanacs, but his story about being a Beatle just doesn't pan out

3. Calls to say he'll pick you up as soon as the standoff with the police is over

2. He's clumsily struggling with the clasp of his own bra

1. He's been on *Geraldo* six times

TOP TEN SIGNS YOU'RE A BAD SURGEON GENERAL

10. You've always got a pack of Luckys rolled up in your sleeve

9. Constantly confusing defibrillator with Fry-O-Lator

8. During swearing in, you vow to do everything in your power "to have Americans dropping like flies"

7. Instead of traditional surgeon general's uniform, you wear a San Antonio Spurs road uniform

6. Never seen in public without a half-empty bottle of Bacardi

5. Instead of flu vaccine, you recommend so-called flu-proof socks

4. Your letterhead contains the phrase "health, schmealth"

3. Often ask yourself, "What would David Crosby do in a situation like this?"

2. You put on an upside-down kitchen colander as your "surgeon general crown"

1. You change warning on side of cigarette package to "I dare you to smoke, you gutless weenie!"

TOP TEN WONDERFUL LITTLE THINGS WE LOVE ABOUT TOM BROKAW

10. Cute way he'll end a really long news story with "Blah blah blah and so on"

9. His hilarious impression of "the Mexican Walter Cronkite"

8. Enjoys a good game of keep-away with Willard's toupee

7. Always leaves the coffee area clean and neat, unlike a certain other network anchor whose name rhymes with "lather"

6. Seeing him in a unitard at annual *Circus of the Stars*

5. His delicious fresh-baked Brokaw Krispie Squares

4. His obvious fondness for furry little "Scoop," the NBC News chinchilla

3. Always has great gossip about Garrick Utley's sex life

2. Those clumsy, splinter-ridden homemade "breadboards" he gives out every Christmas—and is so *proud* of!

1. The haunting fragrance of his Chaz for Men

TOP TEN SIGNS YOU'RE AN OVERWEIGHT COP

10. You're frequently used as a roadblock

9. Instead of yelling, "Freeze!" you yell, "Fritos!"

8. Even patrol car's big block engine can't propel you more than 30 mph

7. You have yet to make it through the Miranda rights without snacking

6. Owner of doughnut shop on your beat is on the Fortune 500 list

5. As you approach your mount, you can hear the horse murmuring, "Please, God, *no!*"

4. Your ass is known as the fourth precinct

3. Suspect you're pursuing on foot has time to stop at a LensCrafters and get new glasses

2. You sometimes work undercover as a sofa

1. You spend a lot of your time trying to apprehend Big Macs

TOP TEN CHRISTMAS MOVIES PLAYING IN TIMES SQUARE

10. *North Poled*

9. *Mrs. Claus and the UPS Guy*

8. *Frosty the Snow Transsexual*

7. *My Little Helper, My Lover*

6. *Well-Hung Ornaments*

5. *Ten Lords-a-Leaping and a Flight Attendant*

4. *I Saw Mommy Nailing Santa Claus*

3. *It's a Wonderbra Life*

2. *Dasher Does Dancer*

1. *Jingle This!*

TOP TEN IRS AGENT PET PEEVES

10. People who fill out their tax forms with mustard

9. Michael Jackson insisting that he's "married"

8. Idiots who pronounce IRS "Urzz"

7. During an audit, when they tape all their receipts into a giant ball and whip it at your head

6. Everybody thinks rock stars get all the action, but the truth is, chicks dig IRS agents

5. Taxpayers who claim their home is a church and they need the big-screen TV to "watch shows about God and stuff"

4. Paranoids who think we're harassing them—like that nut Robert Kessel of 1429 Hillturn Lane, Yonkers, NY (914) 555-2249

3. Letterman claiming that woman who keeps breaking into his house as a dependent

2. When, instead of sending a payment, they just show up at your house with a flyswatter and offer you "two free hours of bug-whackin'"

1. Guys who list your wife under "Entertainment Expenses"

TOP TEN SIGNS YOU'RE GETTING SPECIAL TREATMENT IN PRISON

10. Every night, there's a mint on your pillow

9. Bars of your cell are rusty with Jacuzzi steam

8. Tough new warden says you can have HBO or Cinemax, but not both

7. Each afternoon around 3:00: pony rides!

6. Other prisoners refer to your cell as "Margaritaville"

5. ACLU is looking into why your laundry is soft and fresh—but not *Downy* soft and fresh

4. At 10:00, 2:00, and 4:00 every day: you're mollycoddled

3. You have a summer cell in the Hamptons

2. After lights-out, guards drop by to make s'mores and tell you ghost stories

1. Somehow, you're earning frequent-flier miles

TOP TEN WAYS TO MAKE WORLD CUP SOCCER MORE EXCITING

10. Blindfolds and stilts

9. Give one guy on each team one of them James Bond jet-packs

8. Instead of a soccer ball—the head of actor Judd Nelson

7. Allow goalies to use handguns

6. Have some poor jerk in the middle of the field trying to set up a model railroad

5. Spike Lee on the sidelines talkin' trash

4. Eliminate game itself; let hooligans battle it out on the field

3. Have Sharon Stone inflate the ball

2. Change name of sport to "DEATHBALL 2000"

1. Let 'em use their damn hands!

TOP TEN SIGNS YOUR KID ISN'T COLLEGE MATERIAL

10. His guidance counselor's file consists of two words: Yard work

9. In yearbook was voted "Most Likely to Injure Himself Opening a Door"

8. During algebra class, interrupts teacher and asks, "When do we get to whittle?"

7. Has trouble following those convoluted Three Stooges plotlines

6. At school pep rallies, when the cheerleaders shout, "What's that spell?!" he's always stumped

5. During his appearance on *Jeopardy*, keeps buzzing in and asking, "Alex, can I have some candy?"

4. Consistently beaten in chess by a mealworm

3. You know that little packet of powder that comes with the packing material of a new stereo that says "Do Not Eat"? He eats it.

2. Only high school activities: Dumb Freshmen Club; Dumb Sophomores Club; Dumb Juniors Club; Dumb Seniors Club

1. SAT score? 9

TOP TEN WAYS THE POST OFFICE WILL SPEND THE EXTRA MONEY FROM THE RATE HIKE

10. Hire consultants to plan the *next* rate hike

9. State-of-the-art technology that loses or destroys your mail in a fraction of the time

8. Stamps the size of doormats

7. Scratch 'n' sniff wanted posters

6. Face-lift for Mr. Zip

5. Mail trucks all get musical horns that play "La Cucaracha"

4. Special stamp glue that gives you a three-hour buzz

3. Lobby to put a mailman on Mount Rushmore

2. Prozac and ammo

1. Buy UPS and get them to deliver everything

TOP TEN PET PEEVES OF BOWLING CHAMPION DICK WEBER

10. Malfunctioning hand dryers that suck your arm in up to the elbow

9. Telling people you're a professional bowler and having them ask, "Really? What position do you play?"

8. When the wife won't sleep with you because you missed a 7–10 split

7. You gotta be freakin' Einstein to keep score!

6. When the ol' pinsetter malfunctions, if you know what I mean

5. Trophies where the head of the little bowler looks too much like that Captain Picard guy on *Star Trek*

4. When prankster Earl Anthony fills your ball with pudding

3. Stuck-up royal family of Monaco thinks they can just waltz in and cop your lane—even though it's League Night!

2. Why do miniature golfers get all the chicks?

1. The small minority of tattooed, bad-ass bowlers who spoil the image of the decent, law-abiding majority

TOP TEN SIGNS THE NYPD IS OUT OF CONTROL

10. Emptying service revolvers into doughnut racks just to see which ones have jelly inside

9. You report a murder and they tell you to "Go find Kojak"

8. Crack houses near police stations have been asking them to turn down the stereos

7. Participants in lineups often forced to dress up like Rockettes

6. Instead of sirens, squad cars now blaring "The Beer Barrel Polka"

5. From now on, Tuesday is "Arrest Everyone Named Bob Day"

4. Recently beat cast of Broadway show *Cats* senseless for not having collars and tags

3. Well known that there are no cops on patrol during *Melrose Place*

2. Skeet shooting in midtown with tourists' hats

1. After strip-searching suspects, they say, "Okay, now you do me"

TOP TEN REJECTED
WINTER OLYMPIC SPORTS

10. Alpine Spitting

9. 60-Man Luge

8. Really Drunk Figure Skating

7. Throwing Snowballs at Cars

6. Morbidly Obese Ski Jump

5. Dim-witted Swede Impressions

4. Puck Swallowing

3. Zamboni Demolition Derby

2. Flamboyantly Gay Bobsled

1. Chapping

TOP TEN SIGNS YOU'RE A SHOPAHOLIC

10. You get a daily wake-up call from Sears

9. In State of the Union Address, president thanks you for spurring economic growth

8. You just brained an old lady to get the last pair of five-dollar mittens

7. You live in a tent in the sporting-goods section at Macy's

6. Your last four serious relationships were with mall cops

5. Your name is Sally Johnson and now there's a store called Gap for Sally Johnson

4. You're in a private audience with Pope John Paul II and you ask, "How much for the big hat?"

3. You're neglecting your responsibilities as a workaholic chocoholic news junkie

2. You've dropped, but yet somehow you continue to shop

1. Two words: Visa blisters

KATHIE LEE'S TOP TEN PET PEEVES ABOUT REGIS

10. When he goes on one of her Carnival Cruises, he sneezes on the buffet

9. Every couple of years, just for fun, he switches her birth-control pills with Tic Tacs

8. Never washes or irons her outfits after borrowing them

7. Keeps asking, "Now was it you or your husband who was in the NFL?"

6. Every time he walks, he makes locomotive motions with his arms and shouts, "All aboard the Philbin Express!"

5. Frequently shows up naked at Miss America rehearsal, claiming he's *Mister* Congeniality

4. Always predicting her little Cody will grow up to be a serial killer

3. Joan Lunden this! Joan Lunden that! All he ever talks about is Joan Lunden, Joan Lunden, Joan Lunden!

2. Strains her marriage with all the clumsy passes . . . at Frank!

1. Tells her *regis* means "king" in Latin, and that *kathie lee* means "yammering idiot"

TOP TEN SIGNS YOU'RE NOT A GOOD COMMANDER IN CHIEF

10. Instead of "Hail to the Chief," Marine band plays you on with "Pop Goes the Weasel"

9. The only time you see people in uniform is when you go to McDonald's

8. Can't help giggling when you hear the term "rear admiral"

7. A guy steps on your toe in an elevator and you break down and tell him our nuclear launch codes

6. You tour Fort Benning in a flowing caftan clutching a glass of white wine

5. Whenever there's a 21-gun salute, you dive to the ground and whimper like a terrified puppy

4. You kinda wish you'd been at Tailhook

3. You transfer Bob Hope from USO Entertainment to Advanced Weapons Design

2. You call Japan and ask if it's too late to surrender for World War II

1. Often ask yourself, "What would Gomer Pyle do in a situation like this?"

TOP TEN WAYS TO TELL THE SHOW YOU'RE WATCHING WON'T BE A HIT

10. Laugh track consists of a guy with a wet, hacking cough

9. Show's premise: Man with a bionic ass

8. They announce, "This show was taped in front of a live studio audience . . . at first"

7. It's based on actual cases from the files of the American Dry-Cleaning Institute

6. It's 30 seconds long and extols the goodness of Campbell's soup

5. It's the Weather Channel's very first attempt at a sitcom

4. *TV Guide* listing has a small skull and crossbones next to it

3. Network newsman interrupts broadcast to say, "No bulletin—but can you *believe* this crap?"

2. The actors are holding each other's cue cards

1. During first commercial break, network runs an ad for the show that's replacing it

TOP TEN SURPRISES IN *THE BRADY BUNCH MOVIE*

10. Brady house leaks deadly radon and the family loses their hair and teeth

9. They hunt down the Partridge Family and beat the crap out of David Cassidy

8. Cindy gets grounded for two weeks after firing shots at the White House

7. Gripping scene in which Mom ODs and Dad plunges a hypodermic needle into her heart

6. Ironic twist: The Brady Bill prevents them all from immediately buying handguns

5. All-black cast

4. Produced by the State Department with the proceeds going to bail out Mexico

3. That leg-crossing shot where Alice the maid isn't wearing any underwear

2. Last four hours of movie devoted to family members' theories about the Kennedy assassination

1. They keep gettin' it on with the Osmonds

TOP TEN SIGNS YOUR NEIGHBOR IS A TALK-SHOW HOST

10. At his cookout, "Who wants hamburgers?" is written on a cue card

9. Borrows monologue jokes; never returns them

8. Always asks Domino's Pizza delivery boy if he brought a clip

7. Can sometimes hear his wife Marlo screaming, "You could at least *try* the Grecian Formula!"

6. Invites you over for dinner. Then, when you get there, he tells you you've been bumped

5. Refers to his tank of tropical fish as his "posse"

4. No particular sign—just a statistical likelihood that if you're not a talk-show host, your neighbor is

3. Chases squirrels around the yard with a microphone, screaming, "Is the caller there?"

2. Five words: Applause sign in the bedroom

1. Whenever he leaves, he says, "I'll be right back"

TOP TEN WAYS TO ANNOY A SUPREME COURT JUSTICE

10. Say things like, "Hey, it's one o'clock in the afternoon! Why the hell are you still in your robe?"

9. Bring case titled *Versus* vs. *Versus*

8. When arguing a legal point, begin each sentence with "According to Charo . . ."

7. Eat Exhibit A

6. Say, "I'll approach the bench, as soon as the bench starts using some Binaca!"

5. Steal propeller from their SuperJustice 5000 Hovercraft

4. Whenever there's a quiet moment during a case, groan, "Booooring!"

3. Switch gavel with grand piano; sit back and watch 'em try to pick up a grand piano!

2. Release the robe chiggers

1. When he sentences you to life in prison, just yell, "Screw off!," leave the courtroom, and go have a nice afternoon at the movies

TOP TEN SIGNS YOU'RE NOT GOING TO WIN THE ELECTION

10. Your "motorcade" is down to a rental car and a fat kid on a bike

9. Popular campaign chant of "Four more years!" refers to your prison sentence

8. In the primaries, you finished behind some gag write-in votes for "Ben-Gay"

7. Being first candidate in U.S. history to run an all-mime campaign now seems like a bad idea

6. Ted Koppel matter-of-factly refers to you on the air as "that total dingus"

5. Your campaign manager asks if you've ever thought of selling Amway products

4. It's a stormy flight on your campaign plane; you look out the window, and there on the wing . . . it's Michael Dukakis

3. You're counting on a big last-minute turnout by crack-smoking voters

2. Next week's *TV Guide* lists a time for your concession speech

1. Even you voted for the other guy

TOP TEN SIGNS YOU'RE A TOTAL GEEK

10. You frequently use the words "beam," "me," "up," and "Scotty" in the same sentence

9. Favorite lunch: Kraft Macaroni and Paste

8. You wear tie-dyed clothes and drive a van cross-country following Kathie Lee Gifford's concert tour

7. At your school, your last name has become a slang term for a pimple

6. Spent last six summers at Ross Perot Fantasy Camp

5. Three words: Cherry Kool-Aid mustache

4. Your T-shirt has a photo on it of Amos E. Neyhart, "the Father of Driver's Education"

3. Nobody bothers to pass you the basketball because they know it'll just bounce off your accordion

2. If loving "Ziggy" is wrong, you don't wanna be right

1. You take your Game Boy to the prom

TOP TEN LEAST CONVINCING CRIMINAL ALIBIS

10. "I misinterpreted that NRA slogan about guns not killing people."

9. "It wasn't armed robbery—it was very enthusiastic panhandling."

8. "I was at my weekly poker game at Mother Teresa's place."

7. "I don't even know how to operate a knife."

6. "I was trying on pants at the Gap for Innocent Guys."

5. "I've been hibernating since November."

4. "I was playing 'Simon Says' and the guy who was 'it' said, 'Simon says grab that purse and run for it.'"

3. "My Jacoby & Meyers gift certificate was about to run out."

2. "I was running a sting operation on myself."

1. "Hey! Where am I? How did I get in this courtroom?!"

TOP TEN SIGNS YOU HAVE A DUMB DOG

10. Lengthy pause after "bow" as he tries to remember "wow"

9. When you feed him Alpo, he just eats the meat by-products

8. Buries tail, wags bone

7. On long car trips, likes to stick his head in the glove compartment

6. Spends hours staring at kitchen cabinet, waiting for tiny horses and chuck wagon to come out

5. Has suffered over two dozen concussions from toilet seat falling on his head

4. Thinks "Snausages" is a real word

3. Despite overwhelming evidence, still smokes three packs a day

2. Doesn't lick himself—even though he can

1. Constantly chasing people named "Katz"

TOP TEN REJECTED NAMES FOR *LATE SHOW WITH DAVID LETTERMAN*

10. *Dave's Def Talk Show Jam*

9. *Sally Jesse Letterman*

8. *Tell the Jokes and Watch Them Die*

7. *The All-New Adventures of Necktie Boy*

6. *Cake Challenge 2000*

5. *Bass Fishin' with Dave*

4. *Paul Shaffer & Butthead*

3. *Bonanza*

2. *The Million-Dollar Mistake*

1. *Señor Dave's Fiesta del Cha-Cha*

GENERIC TOP TEN LIST

10. We found Waldo—and he's using a Thighmaster!

9. Dr. Kevorkian's Suicide McNuggets

8. Everywhere you look: groin pulls!

7. Just two more marriages and Liz Taylor wins a mountain bike

6. Three words: Ted Kennedy's pants

5. Insert your own *INSERT YOUR OWN JOKE HERE* here

4. Quayle

3. Madonna put The Club on her cone bra!

2. The Mets suck

1. Oprah Cola

TOP TEN REASONS AMERICA IS THE GREATEST COUNTRY ON EARTH

10. Liberal laws allow you to make millions by spilling McDonald's coffee in your lap

9. Where else could you be a former husband of Cher's *and* a congressman?

8. Visitors from other planets often choose our drunken yokels to take for rides in their UFOs

7. USA much easier to spell than, say, Burkina Faso

6. We produce the vast majority of them *Ace Ventura* movies

5. In New York City, people of all different races and creeds give each other the finger equally

4. We got Yanni

3. Swedes would be lucky to have *one* flavor of Pringles—Hey, Gustav! We've got *ten*!

2. *Yahooo!* A hillbilly chief executive!

1. Two words: Slim Jims

AN END TABLE

Plans by
Master Carpenter

NORM ABRAM

Figure A. Major anatomy and dimensions

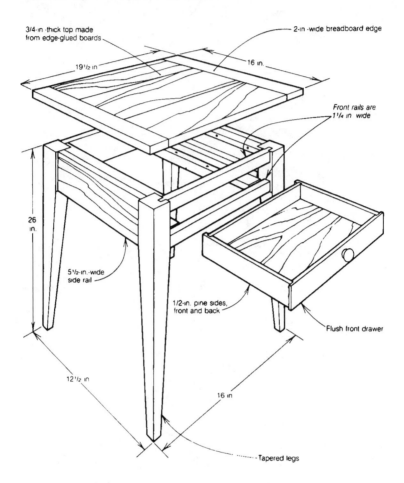

3/4-in.-thick top made from edge-glued boards

2-in.-wide breadboard edge

19½ in.

16 in.

Front rails are 1¼ in. wide

26 in.

5½-in.-wide side rail

1/2-in. pine sides, front and back

Flush front drawer

12½ in.

16 in.

Tapered legs

Figure B. Mortise-and-tenon joinery in legs and rails

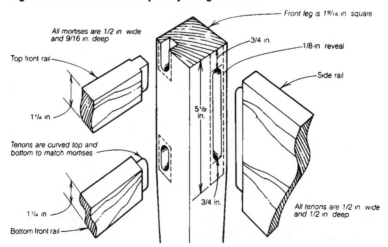

All mortises are 1/2 in. wide and 9/16 in. deep

Front leg is 1⁹/₁₆ in. square

Top front rail

3/4 in.

1/8-in. reveal

1¼ in.

Side rail

5½ in.

Tenons are curved top and bottom to match mortises

1¼ in.

3/4 in.

All tenons are 1/2 in. wide and 1/2 in. deep

Bottom front rail

Figure C. Installing drawer guides and top

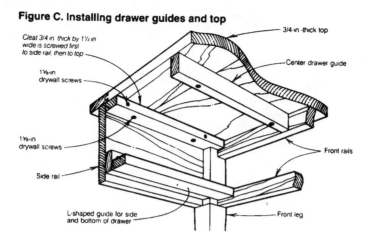

Cleat 3/4 in. thick by 1½ in. wide is screwed first to side rail, then to top

1⅝-in. drywall screws

1⅝-in. drywall screws

Side rail

L-shaped guide for side and bottom of drawer

3/4-in.-thick top

Center drawer guide

Front rails

Front leg

Figure D. Drawer construction details

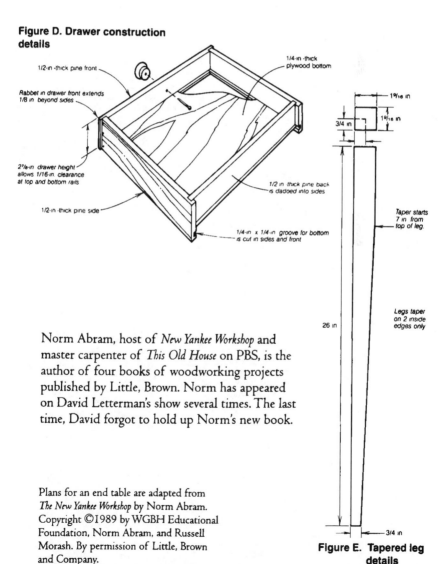

1/2-in.-thick pine front

Rabbet in drawer front extends 1/8 in. beyond sides

2⅞-in. drawer height allows 1/16-in. clearance at top and bottom rails

1/2-in.-thick pine side

1/4-in.-thick plywood bottom

1/2 in. thick pine back is dadoed into sides

1/4-in. x 1/4-in. groove for bottom is cut in sides and front

1⅜ in.

3/4 in.

1⅜ in.

Taper starts 7 in. from top of leg.

Legs taper on 2 inside edges only

26 in.

3/4 in.

Norm Abram, host of *New Yankee Workshop* and master carpenter of *This Old House* on PBS, is the author of four books of woodworking projects published by Little, Brown. Norm has appeared on David Letterman's show several times. The last time, David forgot to hold up Norm's new book.

Plans for an end table are adapted from *The New Yankee Workshop* by Norm Abram. Copyright ©1989 by WGBH Educational Foundation, Norm Abram, and Russell Morash. By permission of Little, Brown and Company.

Figure E. Tapered leg details

Printed in the United States
by Baker & Taylor Publisher Services